Better Homes and Gardens®

mexican
all-time
favorites

Better Homes and Gardens®

mexican
all-time
favorites

WILEY

John Wiley & Sons, Inc.

John Wiley & Sons, Inc.
Publisher: Natalie Chapman
Associate Publisher: Jessica Goodman
Executive Editor: Anne Ficklen
Production Manager: Michael Olivo
Production Editor: Abby Saul
Cover Design: Suzanne Sunwoo
Art Director: Tai Blanche
Layout: Indianapolis Composition
 Services
Manufacturing Manager: Tom Hyland

Test Kitchen

Our seal assures you that every recipe in *Mexican All-Time Favorites* has been tested in the Better Homes and Gardens® Test Kitchen. This means that each recipe is practical and reliable and meets our high standards of taste appeal. We guarantee your satisfaction with this book for as long as you own it.

This book is printed on acid-free paper.

Published by John Wiley & Sons, Inc., Hoboken, New Jersey

For general information on our other products and services or for technical support, please contact our Customer Care Department within the United States at (877) 762–2974, outside the United States at (317) 572–3993 or fax (317) 572–4002.

Wiley also publishes its books in a variety of electronic formats. Some content that appears in print may not be available in electronic books. For more information about Wiley products, visit our web site at www.wiley.com.

Library of Congress Cataloging-in-Publication Data is available upon request.

ISBN: 978-1-4351-2630-5

Printed in China.

10 9 8 7 6 5 4 3 2 1

contents

appetizers
& SNACKS

Sopes, *page 25*

cemitas PUEBLAS MINIS

Prep: 45 minutes
Cook: 4 minutes per batch
Makes: 12 sandwiches

- 1½ **pounds boneless beef top loin steaks**
- ½ **cup all-purpose flour**
- 2 **teaspoons salt**
- 1 **teaspoon ground black pepper**
- 2 **eggs, lightly beaten**
- 1 **tablespoon water**
- ¾ **cup fine dry bread crumbs**
- ¼ **cup vegetable oil**
- 2 **medium ripe avocados, pitted, peeled, and cut up**
- 1 **tablespoon lime juice**
- 12 **egg dinner rolls with sesame seeds (such as challah or brioche), split and toasted**
- 4 **ounces queso panela, queso Oaxaca, or mozzarella string cheese, shredded or pulled into strips**
- ½ **cup thinly sliced red onion**
- ⅓ **cup packed fresh cilantro leaves**
- 2 **to 3 chipotle chile peppers in adobo sauce, chopped***

1 Trim fat from meat. Place meat between two pieces of plastic wrap. Using the flat side of a meat mallet, pound meat lightly until ¼ inch thick. Remove plastic wrap. Cut meat into 12 portions.

2 In a shallow dish, combine flour, salt, and black pepper. In a second shallow dish, combine eggs and the water. Place bread crumbs in a third shallow dish. Dip meat into flour mixture, shaking off excess. Dip into egg mixture, then into bread crumbs, turning to coat.

3 In a large skillet, heat oil over medium-high heat. Cook meat, a few pieces at a time, in hot oil for 4 to 6 minutes or until golden brown, turning once. (Add more oil if necessary during cooking.) Remove meat and drain on paper towels.

4 In a medium bowl, combine avocados and lime juice; coarsely mash with a fork. Season to taste with salt.

5 Spread cut sides of rolls with avocado mixture. Fill with meat, cheese, red onion, cilantro, and chipotle peppers.

Nutrition facts per sandwich: 406 cal., 22 g total fat (5 g sat. fat), 93 mg chol., 684 mg sodium, 30 g carb., 20 g protein.

*****Tip:** Because hot chile peppers contain volatile oils that can burn your skin and eyes, avoid direct contact with chiles as much as possible. When working with chile peppers, wear plastic or rubber gloves. If your bare hands do touch the chiles, wash your hands well with soap and water.

appetizer ALBÓNDIGAS

Prep: 30 minutes
Bake: 14 minutes
Oven: 425°F
Makes: 32 meatballs

1 egg, lightly beaten

1 medium onion, finely chopped

3 tablespoons yellow cornmeal

2 tablespoons snipped fresh cilantro

1 tablespoon finely chopped chipotle chile peppers in adobo sauce (see tip, page 8)

¾ teaspoon dried oregano, crushed

½ teaspoon ground cumin

¼ teaspoon salt

12 ounces ground beef

12 ounces ground pork

½ cup shredded Mexican-style four-cheese blend

32 tortilla chips
Fresh salsa

1 Preheat oven to 425°F. In a large bowl, combine egg, onion, cornmeal, cilantro, chipotle peppers, oregano, cumin, and salt. Add beef and pork. Mix well.

2 Shape mixture into 32 meatballs. Place meatballs ½ inch apart in a 15×10×1-inch baking pan. Bake, uncovered, for 12 to 15 minutes or until done (160°F)*.

3 Remove pan from oven. Using a spatula, push meatballs together so they are touching on all sides. Sprinkle with cheese. Bake for 2 to 3 minutes more or until cheese is melted.

4 To serve, place each meatball on a tortilla chip. Serve with salsa.

Nutrition facts per meatball: 83 cal., 6 g total fat (2 g sat. fat), 23 mg chol., 86 mg sodium, 3 g carb., 5 g protein.

*Tip: The internal color of a meatball is not a reliable doneness indicator. A beef and pork meatball cooked to 160°F is safe, regardless of color. To measure the doneness of a meatball, insert an instant-read thermometer into the center of the meatball.

seasoned GROUND BEEF NACHOS

Prep: 25 minutes
Bake: 5 minutes
Oven: 350°F
Makes: about 40 tostaditas

- 1 **pound lean ground beef or ground pork**
- ⅓ **cup finely chopped onion (1 small)**
- 1 **clove garlic, minced**
- 1 **teaspoon ground cumin**
- 1 **medium tomato, or 3 roma tomatoes, cored and chopped**
- ⅓ **cup finely chopped pitted green olives (such as manzanilla olives)**
- 1 **fresh jalapeño chile pepper, stemmed, seeded, and finely chopped (see tip, page 8)**
- 1 **tablespoon lime juice**
- 1 **tablespoon honey**
- ½ **of a 9.5-ounce package blue corn tortilla chips (about 40 chips)**
- 1 **cup shredded Chihuahua, asadero, or Monterey Jack cheese (4 ounces)**
- 1 **avocado, pitted, peeled, and chopped or mashed slightly**
- ¼ **cup snipped fresh cilantro**
  Salsa (optional)

① Preheat oven to 350°F. For picadillo, in an extra-large skillet, cook beef, onion, garlic, and cumin over medium-high heat until beef is brown and onion is tender, using a wooden spoon to break up meat as it cooks. Drain off fat, if necessary. Stir tomatoes, olives, chile pepper, lime juice, and honey into beef mixture in skillet. Cook over medium-low heat for about 5 minutes more or until juices thicken.

② Spread chips in a single layer on two large baking sheets.* Spoon a generous tablespoon of the picadillo atop each chip. Sprinkle with cheese. Bake for about 5 minutes or until cheese melts.**

③ Transfer chips to a platter. Sprinkle with avocado and cilantro. If desired, serve with salsa.

Nutrition facts per tostadita: 63 cal., 4 g total fat (2 g sat. fat), 11 mg chol., 63 mg sodium, 3 g carb., 3 g protein.

***Tip:** If desired, bake tostaditas in batches to ensure crispy chips and fresh toppings.

****Tip:** Or, if desired, serve ground beef mixture with chips on the side. Sprinkle cheese over warm ground beef mixture. Add avocado, cilantro, and, if desired, salsa.

layered TACO DIP

Prep: 15 minutes
Cook: 10 minutes
Makes: 12 servings

1 **pound ground beef chuck**

¾ **cup water**

1 **1.25-ounce package reduced-sodium taco seasoning**

1 **16-ounce can refried beans**

1 **pound ripe tomatoes, chopped**

6 **scallions, trimmed and chopped (about ¾ cup)**

1 **teaspoon sugar**

½ **teaspoon garlic salt**

¼ **teaspoon ground black pepper**

1 **8-ounce package shredded taco cheese blend**

1 **cup sour cream**

Baked tortilla chips, for dipping

1 Cook ground beef in a large nonstick skillet over medium-high heat for 5 minutes, until browned, stirring occasionally. Stir in the water and taco seasoning. Reduce heat to medium-low and simmer for 5 minutes, stirring occasionally. Stir in refried beans until well combined and heated through. Set aside.

2 In a medium bowl, mix together tomatoes, ½ cup of the scallions, the sugar, garlic salt, and black pepper. In a second medium bowl, mix together 1½ cups of the shredded cheese and the sour cream.

3 In an 8-cup clear bowl, layer half each of the beef mixture, tomatoes, and sour cream mixture. Repeat layering. Scatter remaining ¼ cup scallions and ½ cup cheese over the top. Serve at room temperature with chips.

Nutrition facts per serving: 216 cal., 12 g total fat (7 g sat. fat), 54 mg chol., 537 mg sodium, 10 g carb., 15 g protein.

flautas DE POLLO

Prep: 30 minutes
Bake: 10 minutes
Cook: 3 minutes per batch
Oven: 350°F/300°F
Makes: 10 flautas

½ **cup finely chopped onion (1 medium)**

1 **medium fresh Anaheim chile pepper, seeded and finely chopped (see tip, page 8)**

¼ **cup finely chopped, seeded fresh poblano chile pepper (see tip, page 8)**

3 **cloves garlic, minced**

1 **tablespoon vegetable oil**

12 **ounces cooked chicken, shredded (about 3 cups)**

1 **teaspoon dried oregano, crushed**

½ **teaspoon ground cumin**

¼ **teaspoon salt**

⅛ **teaspoon ground cinnamon**

⅛ **teaspoon ground cloves**

10 **8-inch flour tortillas**

Vegetable oil

Refrigerated fresh salsa (optional)

Mexican crema or sour cream (optional)

Guacamole (optional)

1 Preheat oven to 350°F. In a large skillet, cook onion, chile peppers, and garlic in 1 tablespoon hot oil over medium heat for about 4 minutes or until onion and peppers are soft. Add chicken, oregano, cumin, salt, cinnamon, and cloves; mix well. Set aside.

2 Wrap tortillas in foil and heat in the oven for about 10 minutes to soften. Reduce oven temperature to 300°F.

3 Remove tortillas from oven. Working with one at a time, fill each tortilla with about ¼ cup of the chicken mixture. Roll up tightly and secure with wooden toothpicks.

4 Pour 1 inch vegetable oil into a large skillet. Heat over medium heat to 365°F. Fry flautas, three or four at a time, for about 3 minutes or until crisp and golden, turning once. Remove flautas from oil, being careful to drain oil out of the ends. Drain on paper towels. Keep cooked flautas warm in the oven while frying remaining flautas.

5 Remove wooden picks. If desired, serve flautas with fresh salsa, crema, and guacamole for dipping.

Nutrition facts per flauta: 332 cal., 17 g total fat (3 g sat. fat), 37 mg chol., 465 mg sodium, 30 g carb., 15 g protein.

quesadillas

You can always choose bagged, preshredded Monterey Jack cheese to make quesadillas. But when you get a chance, treat yourself to the authentic taste and texture of a Mexican melting cheese such as asadero, Chihuahua, or queso quesadilla. They provide a Mexican vacation on a plate.

Prep: 20 minutes
Cook: 3 minutes per batch
Oven: 300°F
Makes: 12 servings

- 1 **medium fresh Anaheim chile pepper, or one 4-ounce can diced green chile peppers, drained**
- 1½ **cups shredded asadero, Chihuahua, queso quesadilla, or Monterey Jack cheese (6 ounces)**
- 6 **8-inch flour tortillas**
- 1 **cup shredded cooked chicken**
- ½ **cup chopped, seeded tomato (1 small)**
- 3 **tablespoons finely chopped scallions**
- 1 **tablespoon snipped fresh cilantro, oregano, or basil**

  Purchased guacamole (optional)

  Bottled salsa (optional)

1 Preheat oven to 300°F. If using Anaheim pepper, halve pepper lengthwise; remove seeds and membrane. Cut pepper into thin slivers.

2 Sprinkle ¼ cup of the cheese over half of each tortilla. Sprinkle peppers, chicken, tomato, scallions, and cilantro over cheese. Fold tortillas in half, pressing gently.

3 In a large skillet or on a griddle, cook quesadillas, two at a time, over medium heat for 3 to 4 minutes or until lightly browned, turning once. Remove quesadillas from skillet and place on a baking sheet. Keep warm in the oven. Repeat with remaining quesadillas.

4 To serve, cut quesadillas in half. If desired, serve with guacamole and salsa.

Nutrition facts per serving: 124 cal., 5 g total fat (2 g sat. fat), 24 mg chol., 238 mg sodium, 11 g carb., 9 g protein.

chicken NACHOS

Prep: 35 minutes
Bake: 20 to 22 minutes
Cook: 5 minutes
Oven: 400°F
Makes: 8 servings

2 large bags (14 ounces) tortilla chips

3 tablespoons butter

3 tablespoons all-purpose flour

1¼ cups 2% milk

1 cup shredded pepper Jack cheese

1 14.5-ounce can stewed tomatoes with onion and chiles, drained

1 4-ounce can chopped green chiles, drained

¼ teaspoon salt

¼ teaspoon ground red pepper

1 15-ounce can black beans, drained and rinsed

2 cups shredded, cooked chicken (about 1 pound)

2 scallions, chopped

1 For cheese sauce, melt butter in medium saucepan. Whisk in the flour until smooth. Gradually whisk in the milk until smooth. Cook over medium-high heat until bubbly and thickened, 3 to 4 minutes. Remove from heat. Whisk in cheese until smooth. Stir in tomatoes, chiles, salt, and red pepper.

2 Spread half the chips on ovenproof platter or large pan. Top with half the cheese sauce, half the beans, and half the chicken. Repeat with remaining chips, beans, and chicken. Cover with remaining sauce.

3 Bake for 10 minutes. Cool slightly. Top with chopped scallions. Serve warm.

Nutrition facts per serving: 407 cal., 16 g total fat (8 g sat. fat), 59 mg chol., 566 mg sodium, 45 g carb., 22 g protein.

tex-mex TACO DIP

This super seven-layer dip is piled high with Mexican-style goodies and baked. You'll want to flag this recipe for your next game-day gathering or neighborhood block party.

Prep: 30 minutes
Bake: 25 minutes
Oven: 325°F
Makes: 24 servings

- 1½ **pounds ground turkey**
- 1 **fresh jalapeño chile pepper, seeded and finely chopped (optional; see tip, page 8)**
- 1 **1-ounce envelope reduced-sodium taco seasoning mix**
- 2 **8-ounce packages cream cheese, softened**
- 2 **16-ounce cans refried beans**
- 2 **tablespoons lemon juice**
- 3 **avocados, pitted, peeled, and mashed**
- ½ **cup sour cream**
- ½ **cup mayonnaise**
- 2 **cups shredded cheddar cheese (8 ounces)**
- 2 **cups shredded fresh spinach**
- 3 **medium tomatoes, chopped**
- ½ **cup chopped scallions (optional)**
  Assorted vegetable dippers and/or baked tortilla chips

1 Preheat oven to 325°F. In a large skillet, cook ground turkey and jalapeño pepper, (if using), with half of the taco seasoning mix (about 2 tablespoons) until turkey is no longer pink; remove from heat.

2 Meanwhile, spread cream cheese into the bottom of a 3-quart rectangular baking dish. Spread cream cheese layer with refried beans. Stir the lemon juice into the mashed avocado and spread over refried bean layer. In a small bowl, stir together sour cream, mayonnaise, and remaining taco seasoning mix. Spread sour cream mixture over avocado layer. Top with ground turkey mixture. Sprinkle cheddar cheese over top.

3 Bake, uncovered, for about 25 minutes or until heated through and cheese is evenly melted. Top with spinach, tomato, and (if desired) scallions. Serve with vegetable dippers and/or baked tortilla chips.

Nutrition facts per serving: 243 cal., 17 g total fat (7 g sat. fat), 48 mg chol., 417 mg sodium, 10 g carb., 13 g protein.

cancún BAKED OYSTERS

Prep: 50 minutes
Bake: 8 minutes
Oven: 500°F
Makes: 24 appetizers

4 ounces uncooked chorizo sausage (casings removed, if present)

½ cup minced shallots

½ cup dry white wine (such as Sauvignon Blanc)

8 cups lightly packed chopped fresh spinach

½ cup whipping cream

¼ teaspoon salt

¼ teaspoon ground black pepper

½ cup butter, melted

¼ cup snipped fresh cilantro

2 tablespoons bottled minced garlic (12 cloves)

24 fresh oysters in shells,* shucked and bottom shells reserved

2 fresh jalapeño chile peppers, stemmed, seeded, and finely chopped (see tip, page 8)

2 fresh Fresno chile peppers, stemmed, seeded, and finely chopped (see tip, page 8)

½ to ¾ cup crumbled Cotija cheese or finely shredded Parmesan cheese (2 to 3 ounces)

Lemon and/or lime wedges

Bottled Mexican hot sauce

1 Preheat oven to 500°F. Line a large roasting pan with foil; set aside.**

2 Finely crumble chorizo into a large skillet; add shallots. Cook over medium heat for 5 minutes or until meat is brown and shallots are tender, stirring occasionally. Add wine; simmer, uncovered, until most of the liquid has evaporated.

3 Stir in spinach and cream; cook, uncovered, over medium heat for 10 minutes, stirring occasionally. Stir in salt and black pepper; transfer mixture to a bowl to cool slightly.

4 In a small bowl, combine melted butter, cilantro, and garlic.

5 Place each oyster in a reserved oyster shell; transfer to the prepared roasting pan. Top each oyster with a generous spoonful of the spinach mixture (about 1½ tablespoons). Sprinkle finely chopped chile peppers over spinach mixture; top with cheese. Drizzle each oyster with about 2 teaspoons of the garlic butter.

6 Bake oysters for 8 to 10 minutes or until spinach topping is bubbly and cheese is golden brown. Serve warm with lemon and/or lime wedges and hot sauce.

Nutrition facts per appetizer: 103 cal., 9 g total fat (4 g sat. fat), 27 mg chol., 146 mg sodium, 4 g carb., 3 g protein.

*Tip: Fresh oysters work best in this recipe, but canned ones work, too. If using canned oysters, bake them in small ramekins lightly coated with nonstick cooking spray. Drain the oysters and put two or three oysters in each ramekin.

**Tip: To keep the shells upright while they bake, spread a few cups of rock salt in the roasting pan and nestle the shells into the salt.

triple CITRUS AND SCALLOP CEVICHE

Prep: 30 minutes
Chill: 1 hour
Makes: 16 (¼-cup) servings

1 **pound fresh or frozen bay scallops**

2 **cups lime juice**

½ **cup clam juice**

2 **tablespoons finely chopped canned chipotle chile peppers in adobo sauce (see tip, page 8)**

1 **medium fresh poblano chile pepper, seeded and chopped (see tip, page 8)**

¾ **cup chopped yellow sweet pepper (1 medium)**

1 **medium orange, peeled, sectioned, and chopped**

½ **of a medium grapefruit, peeled, sectioned, and chopped**

1 **medium lime, peeled, sectioned, and chopped**

¼ **cup chopped red onion**

¼ **cup snipped fresh cilantro**

Tortilla chips

1 Thaw scallops, if frozen. Rinse scallops; pat dry with paper towels. Coarsely chop scallops and place in a large nonmetallic bowl. Pour lime juice over scallops; toss to combine. Cover and chill for 1 hour.

2 In a small bowl, whisk together clam juice and chipotle peppers.

3 Drain scallops, discarding liquid. Stir chipotle mixture into scallops. Add poblano pepper, sweet pepper, orange, grapefruit, lime, red onion, and cilantro. Toss to coat.

4 Serve immediately with tortilla chips for dipping.

Nutrition facts per serving: 77 cal., 2 g total fat (0 g sat. fat), 9 mg chol., 136 mg sodium, 10 g carb., 6 g protein.

aguachilis

Prep: 20 minutes
Makes: 6 servings

1½ **English cucumber**

¼ **cup cilantro leaves and stems, coarsely chopped**

2 **tablespoon lime juice**

½ **serrano pepper, seeded and coarsely chopped (see tip, page 8)**

½ **teaspoon salt**

1 **pound peeled and deveined fully cooked shrimp***

½ **of a small red onion, thinly sliced**

1 **medium avocado, pitted, peeled, and sliced**

Cilantro leaves

① Peel, seed, and coarsely chop one cucumber. Reserve the remaining ½ cucumber. In a blender combine the coarsely chopped cucumber, ¼ cup cilantro, lime juice, serrano pepper, and salt. Cover and purée until very smooth. Taste and add additional serrano pepper, salt, and lime juice if needed.

② Slice the remaining ½ cucumber into thin slices.

③ Place some of the puréed mixture in each of 6 serving glasses. Top with shrimp, red onion, avocado, and sliced cucumber.

④ Add additional puréed mixture and garnish with cilantro leaves.

Nutrition facts per serving: 128 cal., 4 g total fat (1 g sat. fat), 147 mg chol., 369 mg sodium, 6 g carb., 17 g protein.

***Tip:** Leave tails attached, if desired.

sopes

Made from corn masa, these little bean-and-cheese-filled boats are the perfect finger food, which means they're great for cocktail parties. Serve them with margaritas, ice-cold Mexican beer, or Mexican sodas.

Prep: 1 hour
Chill: 1 hour
Cook: 1 minute per batch
Makes: 24 sopes

1½ cups masa harina (corn tortilla flour)

3 tablespoons all-purpose flour

½ teaspoon salt

½ cup water

1 egg, beaten

¼ cup shortening, melted

Vegetable oil

Black Bean Filling*

Assorted toppings (such as shredded lettuce, chopped tomato, sour cream, Cotija or Monterey Jack cheese, and/or avocado slices; optional)

1 For dough, in a medium bowl, combine masa harina, all-purpose flour, and salt. Stir in the water and egg. Add melted shortening; mix well. Gently knead dough until it is moist but holds its shape. Cover and chill for 1 hour.

2 Divide the dough into 24 portions. Roll one portion of the dough into a ball (keep remaining dough portions covered to prevent them from drying out). On a well-floured surface, pat ball into a 3-inch round. Form a shell by pinching up the edge of the round to make a ridge. Repeat with remaining dough portions.

3 Pour about ½ inch vegetable oil into a saucepan or deep skillet. Heat over medium heat to 365°F. Fry shells, one or two at a time, for 30 to 60 seconds or until crisp, turning once. Using a slotted spoon, remove shells from hot oil. Drain shells upside down on paper towels.

4 Fill shells with Black Bean Filling. If desired, top sopes with assorted toppings.

*Black Bean Filling: Spoon one 15-ounce can black beans, rinsed and drained, into a medium saucepan. Cook over low heat until heated through. Mash beans slightly with a potato masher or fork. Stir in ¼ cup salsa and ¼ cup chopped fresh cilantro.

Nutrition facts per sope: 113 cal., 8 g total fat (2 g sat. fat), 11 mg chol., 114 mg sodium, 9 g carb., 3 g protein.

Make-Ahead Directions: Prepare and fry as directed above. Place cooled sopes in a single layer in an airtight container. Cover and freeze for up to 1 month. Arrange frozen sopes in a single layer on a baking sheet. Bake for 8 to 10 minutes or until heated through. Fill as directed above.

mexican FONDUE

Prep: 20 minutes
Cook: 3 to 4 hours (low)
    or 1½ to 2 hours
    (high)
Makes: 36 servings

1 14.5-ounce can diced
   tomatoes, undrained
⅔ cup finely chopped onion
½ cup finely chopped
   roasted red sweet pepper
1 4-ounce can diced green
   chile peppers, undrained
3 cups cubed Monterey Jack
   cheese with salsa or
   jalapeño chile peppers
   or regular Monterey Jack
   cheese (12 ounces)
3 cups cubed American
   cheese (12 ounces)
   Assorted dippers (such as
   cubed corn bread* or
   toasted flour tortilla
   wedges)
   Milk

1 In a 3½- or 4-quart slow cooker, combine tomatoes, onion, roasted sweet pepper, and chile peppers. Add Monterey Jack and American cheese; toss gently to combine.

2 Cover and cook on low-heat setting for 3 to 4 hours or on high-heat setting for 1½ to 2 hours. Serve immediately or keep warm, covered, on warm-heat or low-heat setting for up to 2 hours.

3 Serve fondue with dippers, swirling pieces as you dip. If the fondue thickens, stir in a little milk.

Nutrition facts per serving (fondue only): 77 cal., 6 g total fat (4 g sat. fat), 19 mg chol., 236 mg sodium, 1 g carb., 5 g protein.

*Tip: Purchase corn bread or prepare a packaged corn bread mix.

chunky GUACAMOLE

Start to Finish: 20 minutes
Makes: 16 (2-tablespoon) servings

⅔ **cup finely chopped, seeded roma tomatoes (2 medium)**

¼ **cup sliced scallions**

2 **tablespoons lime juice**

1 **tablespoon olive oil**

1 **or 2 cloves garlic, minced**

¼ **teaspoon salt**

⅛ **teaspoon ground black pepper**

2 **very ripe avocados, pitted, peeled, and coarsely mashed**

In a bowl, combine tomato, scallions, lime juice, oil, garlic, salt, and pepper. Gently stir in avocados. Serve immediately or cover the surface with plastic wrap and chill for up to 1 hour.

Nutrition facts per serving: 48 cal., 5 g total fat (1 g sat. fat), 0 mg chol., 39 mg sodium, 3 g carb., 1 g protein.

chili CON QUESO

This popular Tex-Mex dip is a breeze, calling for just a handful of ingredients and taking less than 30 minutes to whip together. If you prefer more spiciness but not too much heat, try the variation using roasted poblano peppers.

Prep: 10 minutes
Cook: 15 minutes
Makes: about 22
     (2-tablespoon)
     servings

½ cup finely chopped onion
   (1 medium)

1 tablespoon butter

1⅓ cups chopped, seeded
   tomatoes (about
   2 medium)

1 4-ounce can diced green
   chile peppers

½ teaspoon ground cumin

2 ounces Monterey Jack
   cheese with jalapeño
   chile peppers, shredded
   (½ cup)

1 teaspoon cornstarch

1 8-ounce package cream
   cheese, cubed

   Tortilla chips or
   corn chips

1 In a medium saucepan, cook onion in butter until tender. Stir in tomatoes, undrained chile peppers, and cumin. Heat to boiling; reduce heat. Simmer, uncovered, for 10 minutes, stirring occasionally.

2 Toss shredded Monterey Jack cheese with cornstarch. Gradually add cheese mixture to saucepan, stirring until cheese melts. Gradually add the cream cheese, stirring until cheese melts and mixture is smooth. Heat through. Serve with chips.

Nutrition facts per serving: 58 cal., 5 g total fat (3 g sat. fat), 16 mg chol., 79 mg sodium, 5 g carb., 2 g protein.

Roasted Poblano Chili con Queso: Preheat oven to 425°F. Line a baking sheet with foil; set aside. Quarter 2 fresh poblano chile peppers lengthwise; remove stems, seeds, and membranes (see tip, page 8). Place pepper pieces, cut sides down, on the prepared baking sheet. Bake for 20 to 25 minutes or until skins are blistered and dark. Bring foil up around peppers to enclose. Let stand about 15 minutes or until cool. Using a sharp knife, loosen edges of the skins; gently pull off the skin in strips and discard. Finely chop peppers. Prepare Chili Con Queso as above, except substitute the finely chopped poblano peppers for the canned diced green chile peppers.

Slow Cooker Directions: Prepare as above. Transfer mixture to a 1½- or 2-quart slow cooker. Keep warm on low-heat setting for up to 2 hours, stirring occasionally.

fresh TOMATO SALSA

Make this version of salsa fresca when summer sun lights the sky and the farmer's markets are fully stocked with tomatoes that ripened on the vine. You can make it as hot as you like, depending on the type and quantity of peppers you use.

Prep: 20 minutes
Chill: 1 hour
Makes: 48 (1-tablespoon) servings

1½ **cups finely chopped tomatoes (3 medium)**

1 **fresh Anaheim chile pepper, seeded and finely chopped, or one 4-ounce can diced green chile peppers, drained**

¼ **cup chopped green sweet pepper**

¼ **cup sliced scallions**

3 **to 4 tablespoons snipped fresh cilantro or parsley**

2 **tablespoons lime juice or lemon juice**

1 **to 2 fresh jalapeño, serrano, Fresno, or banana chile peppers, seeded and finely chopped (see tip, page 8)**

1 **clove garlic, minced**

⅛ **teaspoon salt**

⅛ **teaspoon ground black pepper**

1 In a medium bowl, stir together tomatoes, Anaheim pepper, sweet pepper, scallions, cilantro, lime juice, jalapeño pepper, garlic, salt, and pepper.*

2 Cover and chill for 1 to 24 hours before serving.

Nutrition facts per serving: 10 cal., 0 g total fat (0 g sat. fat), 0 mg chol., 28 mg sodium, 2 g carb., 1 g protein.

Make-Ahead Directions: Spoon the salsa into a storage container. Cover and chill for up to 3 days.

*Tip: For a slightly smoother salsa, place 1 cup of the salsa in a food processor bowl or blender container. Cover and process or blend just until smooth. Stir into remaining salsa.

soups
& STEWS

Adobo Black Bean Chili, *page 38*

ancho-beef STEW

Bake some corn bread to go along with this chunky stew.

Prep: 15 minutes
Cook: 8 to 9 hours (low) or
4 to 4½ hours (high)
Makes: 4 servings

1 **pound boneless
beef chuck, cut into
1-inch pieces**

1 **tablespoon ground ancho
chile pepper**

1 **tablespoon cooking oil**

1 **16-ounce package frozen
stew vegetables**

1 **cup frozen whole
kernel corn**

1 **16-ounce jar salsa**

½ **cup water**

1 Sprinkle beef with ground ancho chile pepper, tossing to coat all sides. In a large skillet, brown beef, half at a time, in hot oil; drain fat.

2 Place frozen stew vegetables and corn in a 3½- to 4-quart slow cooker. Top with beef. Pour salsa and the water over all.

3 Cover; cook on low-heat setting for 8 to 9 hours or on high-heat setting for 4 to 4½ hours.

Nutrition facts per serving: 302 cal., 9 g total fat (2 g sat. fat), 50 mg chol., 842 mg sodium, 28 g carb., 30 g protein.

sopa DE ALBÓNDIGAS

Albóndigas, or meatballs, often are used in soup in Mexico, especially in the beef-producing north. Use the leanest ground meat to avoid extra fat in this "Soup of Meatballs."

Prep: 30 minutes
Cook: 30 minutes
Makes: 6 servings

- 1 **egg or 1 egg white, lightly beaten**
- 3 **tablespoons long grain rice**
- 2 **teaspoons snipped fresh oregano, or 1 teaspoon dried oregano, crushed**
- ¼ **teaspoon salt**
- ⅛ **teaspoon ground black pepper**
- 1 **pound lean ground beef or ground pork**
- 2 **14-ounce cans beef broth**
- 1 **cup water**
- ⅓ **cup tomato paste**
- 2 **cups cubed potatoes (2 medium)**
- 1 **cup thinly sliced carrots (2 medium)**
- 1 **medium onion, thinly sliced**
- ½ **cup frozen peas**

1 For meatballs, in a medium bowl combine egg, uncooked rice, oregano, salt, and pepper. Stir in meat; mix well. Shape meat mixture into 1-inch meatballs.

2 For soup, in a large saucepan combine broth, the water, and tomato paste. Bring to boiling. Add meatballs. Simmer, covered, for 15 to 20 minutes or until meatballs are cooked through.

3 Add potatoes, carrots, and onion to saucepan. Cook, covered, for about 15 minutes more or until vegetables are crisp-tender. Stir in peas; heat through.

Nutrition facts per serving: 259 cal., 9 g total fat (3 g sat. fat), 83 mg chol., 627 mg sodium, 26 g carb., 19 g protein.

Make-Ahead Directions: Mix and shape the meatballs as directed in step 1. Arrange on a baking sheet lined with waxed paper. Freeze until firm. Place meatballs in a plastic freezer bag and freeze for up to 3 months. Thaw in refrigerator before adding to soup.

beef stew IN A POT

This hearty, country-style soup is called mole de olla, *after the earthenware pot, or* olla, *in which it's simmered.*

Prep: 30 minutes
Cook: 1¼ hours
Stand: 30 minutes
Makes: 4 servings

- 12 ounces beef stew meat
- 1 tablespoon cooking oil
- 1 14-ounce can beef broth
- ½ teaspoon salt
- ¼ teaspoon ground black pepper
- 2 to 3 dried ancho chile peppers (see tip, page 8)
- 2 cups chopped, peeled tomatoes (2 large), or one 14.5-ounce can diced tomatoes, undrained
- 1 medium onion, cut up
- 3 cloves garlic, minced
- ½ teaspoon ground cumin
- 2 medium potatoes, cut into 1-inch cubes
- 1 large fresh ear of corn, cleaned and cut crosswise into 1-inch slices, or 1 cup frozen whole kernel corn
- 1 medium zucchini or yellow summer squash, halved lengthwise and cut into 1-inch slices

1 In a 4-quart Dutch oven, brown meat in hot oil. Drain off fat. Add broth, salt, and black pepper to Dutch oven. Bring to boiling; reduce heat. Simmer, covered, for 45 minutes.

2 Meanwhile, cut dried peppers open; discard stems and seeds. Place peppers in a small bowl and cover with boiling water. Let stand for 30 minutes to soften. Drain well. Coarsely chop peppers.

3 In a blender or food processor, combine chopped peppers, tomatoes, onion, garlic, and cumin. Cover and blend or process until nearly smooth. Stir into beef mixture.

4 Add potatoes and corn. Bring to boiling; reduce heat. Simmer, covered, for 20 minutes. Stir in zucchini. Return to boiling; reduce heat. Simmer, covered, for 10 to 15 minutes more or until meat and vegetables are tender.

Nutrition facts per serving: 291 cal., 8 g total fat (2 g sat. fat), 50 mg chol., 741 mg sodium, 32 g carb., 25 g protein.

Make-Ahead Directions: Prepare stew through Step 3. Cool slightly. Cover and chill for up to 2 days. To serve, bring stew to boiling. Continue with Step 4.

adobo black BEAN CHILI

This thick, flavorful chili is packed with nutrients and takes only 20 minutes to prepare!

Prep: 20 minutes
Cook: 20 minutes
Makes: 4 servings

12 ounces 95% lean ground beef

1 medium onion, chopped (½ cup)

1 medium green sweet pepper, chopped (¾ cup)

2 cloves garlic, minced

1 15-ounce can no-salt-added black beans, rinsed and drained, or 1¾ cups cooked black beans

1 14.5-ounce can no-salt-added diced tomatoes, undrained

1 cup frozen whole kernel corn

1 8-ounce can no-salt-added tomato sauce

1 tablespoon canned chipotle chile peppers in adobo sauce, finely chopped (see tip, page 8)

2 teaspoons chili powder

1 teaspoon dried oregano, crushed

1 teaspoon ground cumin

¼ teaspoon ground black pepper

Light sour cream, chopped avocado, shredded cheddar cheese, and/or lightly crushed baked tortilla chips (optional)

1 In a 4-quart Dutch oven, cook ground beef, onion, sweet pepper, and garlic until meat is brown and onion is tender; drain fat. Stir in beans, diced tomatoes, corn, tomato sauce, chile peppers, chili powder, oregano, cumin, and black pepper. Bring to boiling; reduce heat. Simmer, covered, for 20 minutes, stirring occasionally.

2 If desired, serve with sour cream, avocado, shredded cheese, and/or tortilla chips.

Nutrition facts per serving: 308 cal., 5 g total fat (2 g sat. fat), 53 mg chol., 151 mg sodium, 39 g carb., 28 g protein.

mole-style pork AND SQUASH CHILI

It's likely that there are as many versions of mole—a flavorful Mexican sauce—as there are cooks in Mexico. Combining chili powder, cinnamon, and chocolate, the flavors in this intriguing chili are patterned after the brown version of mole.

Prep: 30 minutes
Cook: 30 minutes
Makes: 6 servings

12 ounces boneless pork sirloin chops, cut ½ inch thick

½ cup chopped onion (1 medium)

2 cloves garlic, minced

2 tablespoons olive oil or vegetable oil

2 14.5-ounce cans stewed tomatoes, undrained

8 ounces butternut squash, peeled and cut into ½-inch cubes (about 1½ cups)

1 15-ounce can red kidney beans, rinsed and drained

1 15-ounce can black beans, rinsed and drained

1 cup frozen whole kernel corn

1 cup water

1 tablespoon chili powder

1 tablespoon grated unsweetened chocolate

½ teaspoon ground cumin

¼ teaspoon ground cinnamon

¼ teaspoon dried oregano, crushed

1 Trim fat from meat. Cut meat into ½-inch pieces. In a Dutch oven, cook and stir meat, onion, and garlic in hot oil over medium-high heat until meat is brown. Stir in tomatoes, squash, kidney beans, black beans, corn, the water, chili powder, chocolate, cumin, cinnamon, and oregano.

2 Bring to boiling; reduce heat. Simmer, covered, for about 30 minutes or until meat and squash are tender, stirring occasionally.

Nutrition facts per serving: 289 cal., 9 g total fat (2 g sat. fat), 23 mg chol., 678 mg sodium, 41 g carb., 20 g protein.

pork POZOLE

Prep: 30 minutes
Cook: 2 to 2½ hours
(high)
Makes: 6 servings

1 **15-ounce can yellow hominy, drained**

1 **14.5-ounce can Mexican-style diced tomatoes, undrained**

1 **10-ounce can mild green enchilada sauce**

1 **cup chopped onion (1 large)**

3 **cloves garlic, minced**

2 **teaspoons ground cumin**

1 **1½-pound boneless pork loin (single loin)**

½ **cup snipped fresh cilantro**

1 **tablespoon lime juice**

Sliced avocado

Baked tortilla chips

Fresh cilantro sprigs (optional)

Sour cream (optional)

Lime wedges (optional)

1 In a 3½- or 4-quart slow cooker, combine hominy, tomatoes, enchilada sauce, onion, garlic, and cumin. Add meat; spoon hominy mixture over meat. Cover and cook on high-heat setting for 2 to 2½ hours.

2 Remove meat to a cutting board. Stir the ½ cup snipped cilantro and lime juice into mixture in slow cooker. Coarsely chop meat; return to cooker and stir to combine.

3 Serve topped with avocado. Pass tortilla chips. If desired, garnish with additional cilantro, sour cream, and/or lime wedges.

Nutrition facts per serving: 383 cal., 11 g total fat (2 g sat. fat), 71 mg chol., 652 mg sodium, 32 g carb., 30 g protein.

mexican CHICKEN SOUP

Prep: 30 minutes
Cook: 1 hour
Bake: 20 minutes
Oven: 425°F
Makes: 6 servings

2 to 2½ pounds meaty chicken pieces (breast halves, thighs, and drumsticks), skin removed

6 cups water

2 cups coarsely chopped onion (2 large)

2 cups coarsely chopped celery (4 stalks)

1 cup coarsely chopped tomato (1 large)

½ cup snipped fresh cilantro

1½ teaspoons salt

1 teaspoon ground cumin

¼ to ½ teaspoon cayenne pepper

¼ to ½ teaspoon ground black pepper

1½ cups chopped carrots (3 medium)

1 to 2 fresh poblano chile peppers (see tip, page 8)

Sliced avocado (optional)

Fresh cilantro sprigs (optional)

1 In a 4½-quart Dutch oven, combine chicken pieces, the water, 1 cup of the onion, 1 cup of the celery, the tomato, the snipped cilantro, salt, cumin, cayenne, and black pepper. Bring to boiling; reduce heat. Cover and simmer for 40 to 50 minutes or until chicken is tender. Remove chicken pieces and set aside to cool slightly. Strain the broth mixture, reserving broth and discarding the vegetables.

2 Return the broth to the Dutch oven. Add the remaining 1 cup onion, the remaining 1 cup celery, and the carrot. Bring to boiling; reduce heat. Cover and simmer for about 20 minutes or until vegetables are tender.

3 Meanwhile, preheat oven to 425°F. Line a baking sheet with foil. Cut chile peppers in half lengthwise and remove seeds, stems, and veins. Place pepper halves, cut sides down, on prepared baking sheet. Bake for 20 to 25 minutes or until skins are blistered and dark. Wrap peppers in the foil; let stand for about 15 minutes or until cool enough to handle. Use a sharp knife to loosen the edges of the skins from the pepper halves; gently and slowly pull off the skin in strips. Discard skin. Chop peppers.

4 Remove chicken from bones; discard bones. Chop the chicken. Stir chicken and poblano peppers into broth mixture. Heat through. If desired, garnish with avocado slices and cilantro sprigs.

Nutrition facts per serving: 158 cal., 5 g total fat (1 g sat. fat), 61 mg chol., 638 mg sodium, 7 g carb., 21 g protein.

mexican CHICKEN POSOLE

In parts of Mexico, one day a week is designated as "posole day." Shops and businesses close early and people retire to a temporary posole "restaurant" to enjoy a steaming bowl of this hearty soup. See what all the fuss is about by preparing this quick and easy version.

Start to Finish: 20 minutes
Makes: 4 servings

12 ounces skinless, boneless chicken thighs or breast halves

3 to 4 teaspoons Mexican seasoning or chili powder

2 teaspoons cooking oil or olive oil

1 red or yellow sweet pepper, cut into bite-size pieces (¾ cup)

2 14.5-ounce cans reduced-sodium or regular chicken broth

1 15-ounce can hominy or black-eyed peas, rinsed and drained

Salsa (optional)

Sour cream (optional)

Lime wedges (optional)

1 Cut chicken into 1-inch pieces. Sprinkle chicken with Mexican seasoning; toss to coat evenly. In a large saucepan, cook and stir seasoned chicken in hot oil over medium-high heat for 3 minutes. Add sweet pepper; cook and stir for about 1 minute more or until chicken is no longer pink.

2 Carefully add broth and hominy. Bring to boiling; reduce heat. Simmer, covered, for about 3 minutes or until heated through. If desired, serve with salsa, sour cream, and lime wedges.

Nutrition facts per serving: 192 cal., 8 g total fat (2 g sat. fat), 41 mg chol., 905 mg sodium, 14 g carb., 15 g protein.

chicken AND WHITE BEAN STEW

Refrigerated light Alfredo sauce gives this chicken and bean stew an amazing creaminess.

Prep: 35 minutes
Cook: 4 to 5 hours (low) or
2 to 2½ hours (high)
Makes: 8 servings

2 pounds skinless, boneless chicken thighs

2 teaspoons ground cumin

⅛ teaspoon ground black pepper

1 tablespoon olive oil

2 10-ounce packages refrigerated light Alfredo sauce

1 15-ounce can Great Northern or white kidney beans (cannellini beans), rinsed and drained

1 cup reduced-sodium chicken broth

½ cup chopped red onion (1 medium)

1 4-ounce can diced green chile peppers

4 cloves garlic, minced

¼ cup shredded sharp cheddar cheese or Monterey Jack cheese (1 ounce; optional)

1 Cut chicken into 1-inch pieces. Sprinkle chicken with cumin and pepper. In a large skillet, cook chicken, half at a time, in hot oil over medium heat until brown. Place chicken in a 3½- or 4-quart slow cooker. Stir in Alfredo sauce, beans, broth, onion, chile peppers, and garlic.

2 Cover and cook on low-heat setting for 4 to 5 hours or on high-heat setting for 2 to 2½ hours. If desired, sprinkle each serving with cheese.

Nutrition facts per serving: 360 cal., 16 g total fat (8 g sat. fat), 122 mg chol., 918 mg sodium, 20 g carb., 31 g protein.

chicken AND SALSA SOUP

Chunky bottled salsa provides the heat in this Mexican-inspired soup. It also makes the soup easy enough to whip together for a quick lunch.

Prep: 20 minutes
Cook: 13 minutes
Makes: 4 servings

1¾ cups water

1 14.5-ounce can reduced-sodium chicken broth

8 ounces skinless, boneless chicken, cut into bite-size pieces

1 to 2 teaspoons chili powder

1 11-ounce can whole kernel corn with sweet peppers, drained

1 cup chunky garden-style salsa

3 cups broken baked tortilla chips

2 ounces Monterey Jack cheese with jalapeño chile peppers, shredded (½ cup)

1 In a 3-quart saucepan, combine the water, chicken broth, chicken, and chili powder. Bring to boiling; reduce heat. Simmer, covered, for 8 minutes. Add corn. Simmer, uncovered, for about 5 minutes more. Stir in salsa; heat through.

2 To serve, ladle into soup bowls. Top with tortilla chips and sprinkle with the cheese.

Nutrition facts per serving: 319 cal., 9 g total fat (3 g sat. fat), 42 mg chol., 989 mg sodium, 32 g carb., 20 g protein.

mexican CHICKEN MINESTRONE

You can't beat a tasty, slightly spicy soup that cooks up in half an hour!

Prep: 20 minutes
Start to Finish: 30 minutes
Makes: 6 servings

12 ounces skinless, boneless chicken breast halves, cut into bite-size pieces

1 teaspoon chili powder

2 cloves garlic, minced

1 tablespoon vegetable oil

2 14-ounce cans low-sodium chicken broth

1 cup water

1 15-ounce can black beans, rinsed

1 cup frozen corn

1 cup dried pipette or elbow macaroni

1 14-ounce can Mexican-style stewed tomatoes, cut up

Fresh cilantro sprigs

1 In a bowl, toss chicken with chili powder. In a 4-quart pot or Dutch oven, cook garlic in hot oil over medium heat for 15 seconds and add chicken. Cook, stirring, for 3 minutes.

2 Add broth, the water, beans, and corn. Bring to a boil, stirring frequently. Stir in pasta. Reduce heat and simmer, covered, for 10 minutes or until pasta is tender, stirring occasionally.

3 Stir in tomatoes; heat through. Top each serving with cilantro.

Nutrition facts per serving: 260 cal., 3.5 g total fat (.5 g sat. fat), 33 mg chol., 727 mg sodium, 34 g carb., 22 g protein.

chicken and shrimp
TORTILLA SOUP

Shrimp cook fast (and get overcooked quickly, too), so add them just 3 minutes before you're ready to serve the soup.

Start to Finish: 30 minutes
Makes: 6 servings

- 6 **ounces fresh or frozen medium shrimp**
- 1 **cup chopped onion (1 large)**
- 1 **teaspoon cumin seeds**
- 1 **tablespoon cooking oil**
- 4½ **cups reduced-sodium chicken broth**
- 1 **14.5-ounce can Mexican-style stewed tomatoes, undrained**
- 3 **tablespoons snipped fresh cilantro**
- 2 **tablespoons lime juice**
- 1⅔ **cups shredded cooked chicken breast**
  Crisp Tortilla Shreds*
  Lime wedges (optional)

1 Thaw shrimp, if frozen. Peel and devein shrimp.

2 In a large saucepan, cook onion and cumin seeds in hot oil for about 5 minutes or until onion is tender. Carefully add chicken broth, tomatoes, cilantro, and lime juice. Bring to boiling; reduce heat. Simmer, covered, for 8 minutes. Stir in shrimp and chicken. Cook for about 3 minutes more or until shrimp turn opaque, stirring occasionally.

3 To serve, ladle soup into bowls. Top each serving with Crisp Tortilla Shreds. If desired, serve with lime wedges.

*Crisp Tortilla Shreds: Preheat oven to 350°F. Brush four 6-inch corn tortillas with 1 tablespoon cooking oil. In a small bowl, combine ½ teaspoon salt and ⅛ teaspoon ground black pepper; sprinkle mixture on tortillas. Cut tortillas into thin strips. Arrange in a single layer on a baking sheet. Bake for about 8 minutes or until crisp.

Nutrition facts per serving: 240 cal., 7 g total fat (1 g sat. fat), 76 mg chol., 1356 mg sodium, 21 g carb., 23 g protein.

roasted tomato SOUP

Prep: 35 minutes
Stand: 20 minutes
Cook: 47 minutes
Oven: 425°F
Makes: 6 servings

1 **pound fresh or frozen medium shrimp, peeled and deveined**

2½ **pounds plum tomatoes**

6 **medium fresh poblano chile peppers (see tip, page 8)**

1 **tablespoon olive oil**

1 **large onion, halved and thinly sliced**

3 **cloves garlic, minced**

1 **teaspoon dried Mexican oregano or dried oregano, crushed, or 2 teaspoons snipped fresh oregano**

1 **teaspoon ground cumin**

¼ **teaspoon salt**

3 **14-ounce cans chicken broth**

8 **ounces queso fresco, crumbled**

Snipped fresh cilantro (optional)

1 Thaw shrimp. Set aside.

2 Preheat broiler. Line a 15×10×1-inch baking pan with foil; lightly coat foil with cooking spray. Place whole tomatoes on prepared baking pan. Broil tomatoes 4 inches from heat for 10 to 12 minutes or until skins are charred, carefully turning once halfway through broiling time. When tomatoes are cool enough to handle, peel them over a medium bowl, collecting all of the juices. Remove tomato cores; discard cores and tomato skins. Place tomatoes and juices in a food processor or blender; cover and pulse with several on/off turns until mixture is nearly smooth. Set aside.

3 Preheat oven to 425°F. Halve chile peppers; remove seeds and membranes. Place peppers, cut sides down, in a single layer on a baking sheet lined with foil. Roast about 20 minutes or until skins are blistered and dark. Bring the foil up around peppers to enclose. Let stand for 20 to 30 minutes or until cool enough to handle. Using a paring knife, loosen edges of the skins from peppers; gently and slowly pull off skins and discard. Cut peppers into ½-inch-wide strips.

4 In a Dutch oven, heat oil over medium heat. Add onion; cook for 8 to 10 minutes or until golden brown, stirring frequently. Add garlic, the dried or snipped oregano, the cumin, salt, roasted peppers, and pureed tomatoes. Bring to boiling over medium-high heat. Continue boiling for 7 to 8 minutes or until mixture is quite thick, stirring frequently. Stir in broth. Return to boiling; reduce heat. Simmer, covered, for 30 minutes.

5 Stir in shrimp. Simmer, uncovered, for 2 to 3 minutes or until shrimp are opaque.

6 Ladle soup into bowls. Divide cheese among servings. If desired, sprinkle with cilantro.

Nutrition facts per serving: 283 cal., 7 g total fat (1 g sat. fat), 117 mg chol., 1020 mg sodium, 25 g carb., 29 g protein.

tex-mex beans WITH CORNMEAL DUMPLINGS

Start to Finish: 35 minutes
Makes: 5 servings

- 1 **cup chopped onion (1 large)**
- ¾ **cup water**
- 1 **clove garlic, minced**
- 2 **8-ounce cans no-salt-added tomato sauce**
- 1 **15-ounce can garbanzo beans (chickpeas), rinsed and drained**
- 1 **15-ounce can red kidney beans, rinsed and drained**
- 1 **4-ounce can diced green chile peppers, drained**
- 2 **teaspoons chili powder**
- ¼ **teaspoon salt**
- 1½ **teaspoons cornstarch**
- 1 **tablespoon cold water**
  Cornmeal Dumplings*

1. In a large skillet, combine onion, the ¾ cup water, and garlic. Bring to boiling; reduce heat. Simmer, covered, for about 5 minutes or until onion is tender. Stir in tomato sauce, beans, chile peppers, chili powder, and salt.

2. In a small bowl, stir together cornstarch and the 1 tablespoon cold water; stir into bean mixture. Cook and stir until slightly thickened and bubbly. Reduce heat.

3. Using two spoons, drop Cornmeal Dumplings dough into 10 mounds on top of hot bean mixture.

4. Cover and simmer for 10 to 12 minutes or until a toothpick inserted into the center of a dumpling comes out clean. (Do not lift cover during cooking.)

*****Cornmeal Dumplings:** In a medium bowl, stir together ⅓ cup all-purpose flour, ⅓ cup yellow cornmeal, 1 teaspoon baking powder, and ¼ teaspoon salt. In a small bowl, combine 1 egg white, ¼ cup fat-free milk, and 2 tablespoons vegetable oil. Add milk mixture to cornmeal mixture; stir just until combined.

Nutrition facts per serving: 350 cal., 7 g total fat (1 g sat. fat), 0 mg chol., 803 mg sodium, 61 g carb., 15 g protein.

cha-cha corn CHOWDER

Two kinds of corn give this soup a rich consistency and interesting texture.

Prep: 15 minutes
Cook: 6 to 8 hours (low) or
3 to 4 hours (high)
Makes: 6 servings

3 **medium red potatoes, diced (1 pound)**

2 **14.75-ounce cans cream-style corn**

1 **14-ounce can chicken broth with roasted garlic**

1 **11-ounce can whole kernel corn with sweet peppers, drained**

1 **4-ounce can diced green chile peppers**

¼ **teaspoon ground black pepper**

Cracked black pepper (optional)

Saltine crackers (optional)

1 In a 3½- or 4-quart slow cooker, combine potatoes, cream-style corn, broth, corn with sweet peppers, green chiles, and ground pepper.

2 Cover; cook on low-heat setting for 6 to 8 hours or on high-heat setting for 3 to 4 hours. If desired, top each serving with cracked pepper and serve with crackers.

Nutrition facts per serving: 202 cal., 1 g total fat (0 g sat. fat), 1 mg chol., 898 mg sodium, 49 g carb., 5 g protein.

black bean SOUP

Set out an assortment of toppings—sour cream, chopped avocado, sliced scallions, and/or chopped tomatoes—and warm corn bread to go with the filling soup.

Prep: 25 minutes
Cook: 12 to 14 hours
(low) or 6 to
7 hours (high)
Makes: 6 to 8 servings

1 **pound dry black beans**

12 **cups water**

1 **cup coarsely
chopped carrot**

1 **cup coarsely
chopped onion**

1 **cup coarsely
chopped celery**

2 **large vegetable
bouillon cubes**

2 **teaspoons ground cumin**

2 **teaspoons
ground coriander**

2 **teaspoons dried
savory, crushed**

2 **cloves garlic, minced**

1 **teaspoon chili powder**

½ **teaspoon ground
black pepper**

1 **cup half-and-half or
light cream**

1 Rinse beans. In a large saucepan, combine beans and 6 cups of the water. Bring to boiling; reduce heat. Simmer, uncovered, for 10 minutes. Remove from heat. Cover; let stand for 1 hour. Drain and rinse beans; set aside.

2 In a 4- to 5½-quart slow cooker, combine beans, the remaining 6 cups water, carrot, onion, celery, bouillon cubes, cumin, coriander, savory, garlic, chili powder, and pepper.

3 Cover; cook on low-heat setting for 12 to 14 hours or on high-heat setting for 6 to 7 hours.

4 Mash beans slightly and stir in half-and-half just before serving.

Nutrition facts per serving: 346 cal., 6 g total fat (3 g sat. fat), 15 mg chol., 706 mg sodium, 56 g carb., 19 g protein.

crema DE CALABAZA

Prep: 45 minutes
Bake: 1 hour 10 minutes
Oven: 450°F/325°F
Makes: 4 servings

1 small fresh poblano chile pepper, halved, stemmed, and seeded (see tip, page 8)

1 medium orange

1 pound calabaza or butternut squash, peeled and cut into 1-inch cubes

2 medium onions, cut into 1-inch pieces

1 3-inch sprig fresh thyme

1 1½-inch piece canella or other stick cinnamon

2 tablespoons turbinado sugar

1 tablespoon vegetable oil

4 cloves garlic, peeled

4 whole black peppercorns

2 whole allspice berries

½ teaspoon salt

1 14-ounce can chicken broth

1 cup half-and-half or light cream

Toasted pumpkin seeds (pepitas; optional)

Freshly grated nutmeg (optional)

1 Preheat oven to 450°F. Place chile pepper halves, cut side down, on a foil-lined baking sheet. Bake for about 20 minutes or until skins are charred and blistered. Bring foil up around peppers to enclose. Let stand for 15 minutes. With gloved hands, use a paring knife to peel skins away from peppers; set aside.

2 Using a vegetable peeler, remove the outer peel in wide strips from half of the orange, being careful not to pick up the bitter white pith underneath; reserve peel. Cut orange in half and squeeze halves into a measuring cup to yield ¼ cup juice.

3 Reduce oven temperature to 325°F. In a 15×10×1-inch baking pan, combine orange peel, orange juice, squash, onions, thyme, canella, turbinado sugar, oil, garlic, peppercorns, allspice, and salt. Toss to coat. Roast, uncovered, for 50 to 60 minutes or until squash is tender, stirring once or twice. Discard orange peel, thyme, canella, peppercorns, and allspice.

4 In a blender or food processor, combine half of the squash mixture, half of the broth, and the chile pepper. Cover and blend or process until smooth. Transfer to a large saucepan. Repeat with remaining squash mixture and remaining broth. Stir in half-and-half. Cook and stir over medium heat until heated through (do not boil).

5 Serve in warmed bowls. If desired, garnish with pumpkin seeds and grated nutmeg.

Nutrition facts per serving: 218 cal., 11 g total fat (5 g sat. fat), 23 mg chol., 718 mg sodium, 28 g carb., 4 g protein.

salads
& SANDWICHES

Warm Fajita Salad, *page 64*

taco salad BOWLS

Prep: 35 minutes
Bake: 10 minutes
Oven: 350°F
Makes: 4 servings

- **4** 6- to 8-inch whole wheat or plain flour tortillas
- **12** ounces lean ground beef or ground turkey
- **½** cup chopped onion (1 medium)
- **1** clove garlic, minced
- **1** 8-ounce can tomato sauce
- **1** tablespoon cider vinegar
- **½** teaspoon ground cumin
- **¼** teaspoon crushed red pepper
- **4** cups shredded lettuce
- **¼** cup shredded reduced-fat cheddar cheese (1 ounce)
- **¼** cup chopped green or red sweet pepper (optional)
- **12** cherry tomatoes, quartered

1 Preheat oven to 350°F. For tortilla bowls, wrap tortillas in foil. Heat in oven for 10 minutes. Coat four 10-ounce custard cups with cooking spray. Carefully press 1 tortilla into each cup. Bake for 10 to 15 minutes or until golden and crisp. Cool in custard cups on wire rack; remove bowls from custard cups.*

2 Meanwhile, in a large skillet cook ground beef, onion, and garlic until meat is brown and onion is tender. Drain off fat.

3 Stir tomato sauce, vinegar, cumin, and crushed red pepper into mixture in skillet. Bring to boiling; reduce heat. Simmer, uncovered, for 10 minutes.

4 Place tortilla bowls on four dinner plates. Spoon meat mixture into bowls. Sprinkle with lettuce, cheese, sweet pepper, if desired, and tomatoes.

Nutrition facts per serving: 297 cal., 13 g total fat (4 g sat. fat), 59 mg chol., 575 mg sodium, 23 g carb., 22 g protein.

*Tip: To make tortilla bowls ahead, prepare and cool as directed in Step 1. Place in large freezer container with paper towels between bowls and crumpled around the sides of bowls for protection. Seal and freeze for up to 1 month.

spicy steak SALAD

Prep: 25 minutes
Stand: 10 minutes
Grill: 20 minutes
Makes: 6 servings

- 1 1½- to 2-pound beef flank steak
- Baja Rub*
- 1 tablespoon olive oil
- 3 cloves garlic, minced
- ½ cup beef broth
- ¼ cup lime juice
- ½ to 1 canned chipotle chile pepper in adobo sauce, finely chopped (see tip, page 8)
- 1 teaspoon smoked paprika
- ¼ teaspoon salt
- ¼ teaspoon ground black pepper
- 1 head romaine lettuce, cut lengthwise into 6 wedges
- 2 avocados, pitted, peeled, and thinly sliced
- 1½ cups grape tomatoes, halved lengthwise
- 1½ cups snipped fresh cilantro
- 4 ounces queso fresco, crumbled (1 cup)
- 4 scallions, thinly sliced

1 Score both sides of steak in a diamond pattern by making shallow diagonal cuts at 1-inch intervals. Place beef on a tray or in a dish. Sprinkle Baja Rub evenly over both sides of steak; rub in with your fingers. Let stand for 10 minutes.

2 Meanwhile, for dressing, in a medium saucepan, heat oil over medium-high heat. Add garlic; cook for 30 seconds. Add broth, lime juice, chile pepper, smoked paprika, salt, and black pepper. Bring to boiling; reduce heat. Boil gently, uncovered, for 5 to 7 minutes or until mixture is reduced to ½ cup, stirring occasionally.

3 For a charcoal grill, grill steak on the rack of an uncovered grill directly over medium coals for 17 to 21 minutes or until steak reaches medium doneness (160°F). Remove beef from grill. Cover and set aside. Place romaine wedges on grill rack over coals. Grill for about 3 minutes or until lettuce is wilted and browned, turning once. Transfer to a serving platter or plates. (For a gas grill, preheat grill. Reduce heat to medium. Add beef, and then romaine, to grill rack. Cover and grill as above.)

4 Thinly slice flank steak across the grain. Serve with romaine wedges. Top salads with avocados, tomatoes, cilantro, cheese, and scallions. Pass dressing.

*Baja Rub: In a small bowl, combine 1 teaspoon kosher salt, 1 teaspoon garlic powder, 1 teaspoon smoked paprika, 1 teaspoon ground black pepper, ½ teaspoon ground cumin, and ¼ to ½ teaspoon cayenne pepper. Mix well.

Nutrition facts per serving: 342 cal., 20 g total fat (6 g sat. fat), 46 mg chol., 609 mg sodium, 14 g carb., 30 g protein.

warm fajita SALAD

All the sizzling goodness of lime-and-cilantro-flavored beef strips combined with cool, crisp greens makes for a sensational salad for lunch or dinner.

Start to Finish: 35 minutes
Oven: 400°F
Makes: 4 servings

- 12 ounces boneless beef top sirloin steak
- ¼ cup lime juice
- ¼ cup reduced-sodium chicken broth
- 1 tablespoon snipped fresh cilantro
- 1½ teaspoons cornstarch
- 2 cloves garlic, minced
- ½ teaspoon ground cumin
- ¼ teaspoon salt
- ¼ teaspoon ground black pepper
- 2 small green, red, and/or yellow sweet peppers, seeded and cut into thin strips
- 2 small onions, cut into thin wedges
- 1 tablespoon vegetable oil
- 1 10-ounce package torn mixed salad greens
- 12 cherry tomatoes, halved or quartered
- Baked Tortilla Strips*

1 If desired, partially freeze meat for easier slicing. Trim fat from meat. Cut meat into thin bite-size strips. For sauce, in a small bowl combine lime juice, broth, cilantro, cornstarch, and garlic; set aside. Sprinkle meat strips with cumin, salt, and black pepper; toss to coat.

2 Coat a large skillet with cooking spray. Preheat over medium-high heat. Add sweet peppers and onions; cook and stir for 3 to 4 minutes or until crisp-tender. Remove from skillet. Pour oil into hot skillet. Add meat; cook and stir for 2 to 3 minutes or until meat is slightly pink in center. Push meat from center of skillet.

3 Stir sauce; add to center of skillet. Cook and stir until thickened and bubbly. Return cooked vegetables to skillet. Stir all ingredients together to coat with sauce. Cook and stir until heated through.

4 To serve, divide salad greens and tomatoes among four dinner plates. Spoon meat mixture on top of greens mixture. Sprinkle with Baked Tortilla Strips.

*Baked Tortilla Strips: Preheat oven to 400°F. Cut 1 corn tortilla into ⅛- to ¼-inch strips; cut long strips in half crosswise. Place strips on ungreased baking sheet. Coat with nonstick cooking spray; sprinkle lightly with paprika and chili powder. Bake for about 8 minutes or until strips are golden and crisp, stirring once.

Nutrition facts per serving: 200 cal., 8 g total fat (2 g sat. fat), 52 mg chol., 246 mg sodium, 14 g carb., 21 g protein.

24-hour CHICKEN FIESTA SALAD

Chilling the salad for up to 24 hours allows the flavors to blend. Layer the ingredients one evening and have a ready-to-serve meal the next.

Prep: 30 minutes
Chill: 4 to 24 hours
Makes: 4 servings

- **4 cups torn iceberg, Boston, or Bibb lettuce**
- **½ cup shredded Monterey Jack cheese with jalapeño chile peppers (2 ounces)**
- **1 8-ounce can red kidney beans, rinsed and drained, or 12 ounces of a 15-ounce can garbanzo beans, rinsed and drained (1 cup)**
- **1½ cups chopped cooked chicken or turkey (about 8 ounces)**
- **2 small tomatoes, cut into thin wedges**
- **½ of a small jicama (about 4 ounces), cut into bite-size strips (1 cup), or 1 cup shredded carrot**
- **½ cup sliced pitted black olives (optional)**
- **Chile Dressing***
- **¾ cup crushed tortilla chips (optional)**

Place the lettuce in a large (2-quart) salad bowl. Layer ingredients in the following order: cheese, beans, chicken, tomatoes, jicama, and, if desired, olives. Spread Chile Dressing evenly over salad, sealing to edge of bowl. Cover salad tightly with plastic wrap. Chill for 4 to 24 hours. To serve, toss lightly to coat evenly. If desired, sprinkle with crushed tortilla chips.

*Chile Dressing: In a small bowl, stir together ½ cup mayonnaise or salad dressing, one 4-ounce can chopped canned green chile peppers, 1½ teaspoons chili powder, and 1 clove garlic, minced. Makes about ¾ cup.

Nutrition facts per serving: 444 cal., 32 g total fat (7 g sat. fat), 73 mg chol., 460 mg sodium, 17 g carb., 26 g protein.

mexican SALAD PLATTER

Start to Finish: 30 minutes
Makes: 6 servings

¼ cup olive oil or
   vegetable oil

3 tablespoons cider vinegar

3 tablespoons snipped
   fresh cilantro

1 canned chipotle chile
   pepper in adobo sauce,
   drained and finely
   chopped (see tip,
   page 8)

1 clove garlic, minced

½ teaspoon salt

10 cups coarsely shredded
   lettuce (about 1 large
   head iceberg or
   romaine lettuce)

3½ cups shredded
   cooked chicken*

10 grape tomatoes, halved

¼ cup sliced scallions

1 avocado, pitted, peeled,
   and sliced

   Corn and Black Bean
   Relish,** or one
   16-ounce jar corn and
   black bean salsa

1 lime, cut into wedges
   and halved

1 For dressing, in a screw-top jar combine oil, vinegar, cilantro, chile pepper, garlic, and salt. Cover and shake well to combine; set aside.

2 Cover a large serving platter with lettuce. Toss chicken with 1 tablespoon of the dressing. In a small bowl, combine tomatoes and scallions. Arrange tomato mixture, sliced avocado, chicken mixture, Corn and Black Bean Relish, and lime wedges in vertical rows on top of lettuce on platter. To serve, drizzle with the remaining dressing.

**Corn and Black Bean Relish: In a small mixing bowl, combine one 15-ounce can black beans, rinsed and drained; ¾ cup cooked fresh or frozen whole kernel corn; and 1 small orange or green sweet pepper, chopped (optional). Toss with 2 tablespoons of the dressing.

Nutrition facts per serving: 365 cal., 19 g total fat (3 g sat. fat), 73 mg chol., 466 mg sodium, 22 g carb., 31 g protein.

Make-Ahead Directions: Prepare salad as directed, except toss avocado slices with 1 tablespoon lime juice to prevent avocado from browning. Do not drizzle salad with remaining dressing until just before serving. Cover and chill salad and dressing for up to 1 hour.

*Tip: A deli-roasted chicken offers a good choice to use for cooked shredded chicken.

turkey-jicama SALAD WITH LIME DRESSING

Prep: 45 minutes
Marinate: 2 hours
Grill: 18 minutes
Stand: 10 minutes
Makes: 6 servings

½ cup snipped fresh cilantro

⅓ cup lime juice

⅓ cup olive oil

¾ teaspoon ground cumin

¼ teaspoon salt

⅛ teaspoon cayenne pepper

1½ pounds turkey breast tenderloins

6 cups packaged mixed salad greens

1 small jicama, cut into bite-size strips (about 3 cups)

1 bunch radishes, trimmed and thinly sliced* (about 2 cups)

½ of a small red onion, thinly sliced

1 avocado, pitted, peeled, and sliced

1 mango, peeled, pitted, and sliced, or 1 cup drained refrigerated mango slices

⅓ cup pumpkin seeds (pepitas), toasted

1 For dressing, in a screw-top jar combine cilantro, lime juice, oil, cumin, salt, and cayenne. Cover and shake well to combine. Transfer ¼ cup of the dressing to a large resealable plastic bag set in a shallow bowl. Add turkey tenderloins to bag. Seal bag; turn to coat tenderloins. Marinate in the refrigerator for 2 to 4 hours, turning bag occasionally. Cover and chill remaining dressing.

2 Drain turkey, discarding marinade. For a charcoal grill, grill turkey on the rack of an uncovered grill directly over medium coals for 18 to 22 minutes or until turkey is no longer pink (170°F), turning once halfway through grilling. (For a gas grill, preheat grill. Reduce heat to medium. Place turkey on grill rack over heat. Cover and grill as above.)

3 Remove turkey from grill and let stand for 10 minutes. In a very large bowl combine salad greens, jicama, radishes, and red onion. Add most of the chilled dressing; toss to coat. Arrange on a large serving platter. Top with avocado and mango. Thinly slice the turkey and place on greens. Drizzle with the remaining chilled dressing. Sprinkle with pumpkin seeds.

Nutrition facts per serving: 403 cal., 22 g total fat (3 g sat. fat), 70 mg chol., 186 mg sodium, 20 g carb., 34 g protein.

*Tip: Use a food processor to quickly slice the radishes.

lobster, mango, AND
ROASTED CORN LETTUCE CUPS

Start to Finish: 30 minutes
Makes: 8 servings

- ¼ **cup olive oil**
- 1 **tablespoon bottled minced garlic (6 cloves)**
- ¼ **teaspoon salt**
- ¼ **teaspoon chili powder**
- ¼ **cup lime juice**
- 1 **cup fresh or frozen whole kernel corn**
- 3 **cups cooked lobster tail and claw meat,* chopped (two 1½-pound lobsters)**
- 1½ **cups chopped fresh mango**
- ¾ **cup snipped fresh cilantro**
- ½ **cup chopped red sweet pepper (1 small)**
- ½ **cup finely chopped red onion**
- ½ **cup mayonnaise or salad dressing**
- 2 **fresh jalapeño chile peppers, stemmed, seeded, and finely chopped (see tip, page 8)**
  Salt and ground black pepper
- 8 **leaves butterhead (Boston or Bibb) lettuce (about 1 head)**
- ¼ **cup pumpkin seeds (pepitas), toasted**

1 For vinaigrette, in a small skillet, cook oil, garlic, the ¼ teaspoon salt, and the chili powder over medium heat for 1 to 2 minutes or until garlic sizzles. Whisk in lime juice. Remove from heat and set aside.

2 Preheat a large nonstick skillet over medium-high heat. Add corn to hot skillet; cook, without stirring, for 2 to 3 minutes or until kernels are browned and roasted on one side (be careful, because corn will pop and sputter). Stir and cook for 1 minute more. Transfer corn to a large bowl.

3 Add lobster, mango, cilantro, sweet pepper, onion, mayonnaise, and chile peppers to corn, stirring to combine. Season to taste with salt and pepper.

4 To serve, place a lettuce leaf in each of eight large goblets or small serving dishes. Spoon lobster mixture onto lettuce leaves. Sprinkle with pepitas and drizzle with vinaigrette.

Nutrition facts per serving: 311 cal., 22 g total fat (4 g sat. fat), 51 mg chol., 471 mg sodium, 14 g carb., 17 g protein.

*Tip: Steamed, broiled, or grilled lobster meat works well in this recipe.

chayote SALAD

Call it the wily chayote. It has the look of a pear and a texture and taste somewhere between a cucumber and a zucchini, yet in the company of sugar and cinnamon, it acts like an apple.

Prep: 30 minutes
Marinate: 3 hours
Makes: 6 side-dish
servings

- 3 medium chayotes, peeled, pitted, and coarsely chopped
- 1 cup canned garbanzo beans, rinsed and drained
- ¼ cup lemon juice
- ¼ cup olive oil or salad oil
- ¼ cup water
- 1 tablespoon snipped fresh basil, or 1 teaspoon dried basil, crushed
- ½ teaspoon sugar
- ¼ teaspoon salt
- 2 cloves garlic, minced
- ¼ cup sliced pitted black olives
- 6 lettuce leaves
- 2 medium tomatoes, cut into wedges

Thinly sliced red onion

1 In a medium saucepan, cook chayotes, covered, in a small amount of boiling salted water for 5 to 6 minutes or until tender; drain. Rinse with cold water to stop cooking; drain well. Transfer to a medium bowl; add garbanzo beans.

2 For marinade, in a screw-top jar combine lemon juice, oil, water, basil, sugar, salt, and garlic. Cover and shake well. Pour marinade over chayote mixture, stirring to coat well. Cover and marinate in the refrigerator for 3 to 24 hours, stirring occasionally.

3 To serve, drain chayote mixture, reserving marinade. Stir in olives. Spoon chayote mixture onto six lettuce-lined plates. Top each serving with tomato wedges and red onion. Drizzle with some of the reserved marinade.

Nutrition facts per serving: 170 cal., 10 g total fat (1 g sat. fat), 0 mg chol., 273 mg sodium, 18 g carb., 3 g protein.

layered taco SALAD

For a spicier version of this pretty tiered salad, use Monterey Jack with chile peppers.

Prep: 20 minutes
Chill: 2 hours
Makes: 4 servings

1 **15-ounce can black beans, rinsed and drained**

4 **cups shredded iceberg lettuce**

1 **medium tomato, seeded and chopped**

1½ **cups shredded cheddar or Monterey Jack cheese**

¼ **cup sliced pitted black olives**

¼ **cup sliced scallions**

1 **6-ounce carton frozen avocado dip, thawed**

½ **cup sour cream**

1 **4-ounce can chopped green chile peppers, drained**

1 **tablespoon milk**

1 **clove garlic, minced**

½ **teaspoon chili powder**

Chopped tomato (optional)

2 **cups coarsely crushed tortilla chips**

1 In a 2½-quart glass salad bowl, layer black beans, lettuce, tomato, cheese, olives, and scallions.

2 For dressing, in a medium bowl stir together avocado dip, sour cream, chile peppers, milk, garlic, and chili powder. Spread over the top of the salad. If desired, sprinkle with chopped tomato. Cover the surface with plastic wrap and chill for at least 2 hours or up to 24 hours.

3 Before serving, toss salad together and serve over crushed tortilla chips.

Nutrition facts per serving: 561 cal., 40 g total fat (14 g sat. fat), 58 mg chol., 1277 mg sodium, 37 g carb., 24 g protein.

festive TACO BURGERS

Flour tortillas replace the hamburger buns in this recipe to make these taco burgers twice the fun!

Prep: 25 minutes
Broil: 10 minutes
Oven: 350°F/broil
Makes: 5 servings

- 1 **cup finely chopped tomato**
- ¼ **cup green or red taco sauce**
- 2 **tablespoons snipped fresh cilantro**
- 5 **8- to 10-inch flour tortillas**
- 1 **4-ounce can diced green chile peppers**
- ¼ **cup fine dry bread crumbs**
- ¼ **cup finely chopped scallions**
- 1 **teaspoon dried oregano, crushed**
- ½ **teaspoon ground cumin**
- ¼ **teaspoon ground black pepper**
- ⅛ **teaspoon salt**
- 1 **pound ground beef**
- 1 **cup shredded lettuce or red cabbage**

1 Preheat oven to 350°F. In a medium bowl, stir together tomato, taco sauce, and cilantro. Cover and set aside. Wrap tortillas in aluminum foil; bake for 10 minutes. Remove from oven, but do not open foil packet.

2 Meanwhile, in a large bowl stir together undrained chili peppers, bread crumbs, scallions, oregano, cumin, black pepper, and salt until well mixed. Add meat and mix well. Shape mixture into 5 oval patties about 4 inches long and ½ inch thick. Lightly coat the unheated rack of a broiler pan with cooking spray; arrange patties on broiler pan. Broil 4 inches from the heat for 10 to 12 minutes or until done (160°F), turning halfway through broiling time.

3 To serve, place a patty on each warm tortilla; spoon shredded lettuce and tomato mixture over each patty. Wrap tortillas around patties.

Nutrition facts per serving: 304 cal., 14 g total fat (5 g sat. fat), 57 mg chol., 514 mg sodium, 22 g carb., 21 g protein.

pork and sweet POTATO EMPANADAS

Prep: 55 minutes
Bake: 20 minutes
Oven: 425°F
Makes: 8 empanadas

- 1 **pound ground pork**
- ½ **cup chopped onion (1 medium)**
- 3 **cloves garlic, minced**
- 1½ **cups peeled and chopped sweet potato**
- 1 **8-ounce can tomato sauce**
- ¼ **cup raisins**
- 1 **teaspoon ground pasilla chile pepper or ancho chile pepper**
- ½ **teaspoon dry mustard**
- ½ **teaspoon ground cumin**
- ¼ **teaspoon salt**
- 3 **cups all-purpose flour**
- ½ **teaspoon salt**
- ½ **cup shortening**
- ¼ **cup butter**
- ½ **cup milk**
- 2 **eggs**
- 1 **tablespoon water**

1 For filling, in a large skillet cook pork, onion, and garlic over medium heat until pork is brown, using a wooden spoon to break up meat as it cooks. Drain off fat. Stir sweet potato, tomato sauce, raisins, ground chile pepper, mustard, cumin, and the ¼ teaspoon salt into pork mixture in skillet. Bring to boiling; reduce heat. Simmer, covered, for 10 to 12 minutes or until sweet potatoes are tender, stirring occasionally.

2 For pastry, in a large bowl combine flour and the ½ teaspoon salt. Using a pastry blender, cut in shortening and butter until mixture resembles coarse crumbs. In a small bowl, beat together the ½ cup milk and one of the eggs with a fork. Add the milk mixture to the flour mixture; stir until combined. If dough seems too dry, add enough additional milk (1 to 2 tablespoons) to make a dough that is easy to handle. Turn dough out onto a lightly floured surface; shape into a ball. Divide dough into eight portions.

3 Preheat oven to 425°F. On a lightly floured surface, roll each portion of dough into a 6-inch circle. Place about ½ cup of filling in the center of each dough circle. Brush edge of each dough circle with milk; fold dough circle in half, pinching edge to seal. If desired, press edge with tines of a fork. Place filled empanadas on an ungreased baking sheet.

4 In a small bowl, place remaining egg and water; beat together using a fork. Brush egg mixture over empanadas. Prick tops with tines of a fork. Bake for about 20 minutes or until empanadas are golden brown and heated through.

Nutrition facts per empanada: 558 cal., 32 g total fat (12 g sat. fat), 110 mg chol., 483 mg sodium, 49 g carb., 18 g protein.

grilled chicken MOLE
SANDWICHES

Prep: 30 minutes
Grill: 12 minutes
Makes: 4 sandwiches

- 3 dried New Mexico chile peppers or pasilla chile peppers (see tip, page 8)
- ¼ cup chopped onion
- 3 cloves garlic, chopped
- 1 tablespoon vegetable oil
- ½ cup water
- 3 tablespoons chopped Mexican-style sweet chocolate or semisweet chocolate
- 4 skinless, boneless chicken breast halves (about 1¼ pounds total)

  Salt
- 1 small avocado, pitted, peeled, and mashed
- 2 tablespoons light mayonnaise or salad dressing
- ¼ teaspoon cayenne pepper
- ⅛ teaspoon salt
- 4 6-inch bolitos, bolillos, or other Mexican rolls or hard rolls, split

  Leaf lettuce leaves (optional)

  Tomato slices (optional)

  Papaya slices (optional)

1 For mole, halve chile peppers; remove stems and seeds. Coarsely chop peppers; set aside. In a large skillet cook onion and garlic in hot oil over medium-high heat until onion is tender. Add the dried peppers and the water. Reduce heat to medium. Stir in chocolate. Cook and stir, uncovered, for 3 to 5 minutes or until thickened and bubbly; cool slightly. Transfer mixture to a food processor or blender; cover and process or blend until mixture forms a smooth paste. Set aside to cool. Reserve 1 to 2 tablespoons of the mole.

2 Sprinkle chicken with salt. Using a sharp knife, carefully cut a horizontal slit two-thirds of the way through each breast half. Spread inside surfaces of the chicken with cooled mole; fold closed. Rub outside surfaces with reserved 1 to 2 tablespoons mole.

3 For a charcoal grill, grill chicken on greased rack of an uncovered grill directly over medium coals for 12 to 15 minutes or until chicken is tender and no longer pink (170°F), turning once halfway through grilling. (For a gas grill, preheat grill. Reduce heat to medium. Place chicken on greased grill rack over heat. Cover and grill as above.) Slice chicken.

4 Meanwhile, in a small bowl stir together avocado, mayonnaise, cayenne, and the ⅛ teaspoon salt.

5 To assemble sandwiches, spread avocado mixture on cut sides of rolls. Fill with chicken and, if desired, lettuce, tomato, and papaya.

Nutrition facts per sandwich: 512 cal., 19 g total fat (2 g sat. fat), 85 mg chol., 657 mg sodium, 44 g carb., 40 g protein.

turkey-mango
QUESADILLAS

Start to Finish: 30 minutes
Oven: 250°F
Makes: 4 servings

4 **8-inch flour tortillas**

1 **tablespoon vegetable oil**

6 **ounces Gouda or smoked Gouda cheese, thinly sliced or shredded**

8 **ounces cooked or smoked turkey or chicken, chopped**

½ **cup bottled roasted red sweet peppers, drained and sliced**

1 **cup mango salsa or mango-peach salsa**

¼ **cup snipped fresh cilantro (optional)**

1 Preheat oven to 250°F. Brush one side of each tortilla with some of the oil. Place tortillas, oil side down, on extra-large baking sheet. Top half of each tortilla with cheese, turkey, red peppers, half the salsa, and the cilantro. Fold tortillas in half; press gently.

2 In 12-inch skillet, cook quesadillas, two at a time, over medium heat for 6 minutes until lightly browned and crisp, turning once. Place cooked quesadillas on baking sheet; keep warm in oven while cooking remaining quesadillas.

3 To serve, cut in wedges. Pass remaining salsa.

Nutrition facts per serving: 392 cal., 18 g total fat (9 g sat. fat), 96 mg chol., 778 mg sodium, 27 g carb., 32 g protein.

mexican TUNA MELT

Start to Finish: 20 minutes
Makes: 4 servings

- 2 **6-ounce cans chunk white tuna, drained**
- ¼ **cup mayonnaise or salad dressing**
- 2 **tablespoons toasted pumpkin seeds (pepitas)* or dry-roasted sunflower seeds**
- ½ **teaspoon finely shredded lime zest**
- 1 **tablespoon lime juice**
- 1 **tablespoon finely chopped red onion**
- 1 **teaspoon finely chopped chipotle chile peppers in adobo sauce (optional; see tip, page 8)**
- 8 **slices whole wheat bread**
- 4 **ounces Monterey Jack cheese with jalapeño chile peppers, shredded**
- 1 **small tomato, thinly sliced**
- 1 **cup shredded lettuce**

Preheat broiler. In a medium bowl, combine tuna, mayonnaise, pumpkin seeds, lime zest, lime juice, onion, and, if desired, chipotle. Place 4 of the bread slices on a baking sheet. Spread the tuna mixture on the bread slices. Top with cheese. Broil 4 to 5 inches from the heat for 1½ to 3 minutes or until cheese melts. Top with tomato slices, lettuce, and remaining bread slices.

Nutrition facts per serving: 467 cal., 26 g total fat (9 g sat. fat), 73 mg chol., 883 mg sodium, 24 g carb., 36 g protein.

*Tip: To toast pumpkin seeds, spread seeds in a shallow baking pan; bake in a 350°F oven for 7 to 10 minutes or until toasted. Cool.

mexican VEGETABLE SANDWICH

Start to Finish: 20 minutes
Makes: 4 servings

⅓ cup mayonnaise

2 to 3 teaspoons finely chopped chipotle chile peppers in adobo sauce (see tip, page 8)

2 teaspoons lime juice

4 French rolls, split and toasted, if desired

2 4-ounce cans whole green chiles, drained

1 medium avocado, pitted, peeled, and sliced

1 medium tomato, sliced

¼ cup thinly sliced red onion

4 slices Monterey Jack cheese

1 In a small bowl, combine mayonnaise, chipotle, and lime juice.

2 Spread both sides of each roll with mayonnaise mixture. Split whole chiles so they lay flat. Top bottom half of each roll with green chiles, avocado, tomato, red onion, and Monterey Jack cheese. Add top halves of rolls.

Nutrition facts per serving: 420 cal., 30 g total fat (9 g sat. fat), 32 mg chol., 722 mg sodium, 27 g carb.,12 g protein.

queso fresco QUESADILLAS WITH PAPAYA SALSA

Prep: 25 minutes
Chill: 2 hours
Cook: 8 minutes
Makes: 4 servings

- 1 medium papaya, peeled, pitted, and chopped (2 cups)
- 3 tablespoons lime juice
- 2 tablespoons thinly sliced scallion
- 2 tablespoons finely chopped red sweet pepper
- 2 tablespoons snipped fresh cilantro
- 1 tablespoon packed brown sugar
- 1 teaspoon bottled hot pepper sauce
- ½ teaspoon grated fresh ginger
- ¼ teaspoon salt
- 4 ounces queso fresco, crumbled (1 cup)
- 4 ounces Monterey Jack cheese, shredded (1 cup)
- 8 6-inch corn tortillas

1 For papaya salsa, in a medium bowl combine papaya, lime juice, scallion, red sweet pepper, 1 tablespoon of the cilantro, the brown sugar, hot pepper sauce, ginger, and salt. Mix well. Cover and refrigerate for 2 hours before serving.

2 In a medium bowl, combine queso fresco, Monterey Jack cheese, and the remaining 1 tablespoon cilantro. Divide cheese mixture evenly among four of the tortillas. Top each with a remaining tortilla; press firmly.

3 Lightly oil a large skillet or griddle; heat over medium heat. Place a filled quesadilla in skillet or on griddle; cook for 2 to 4 minutes or until golden and cheese starts to melt, turning once.

4 Cut quesadillas into quarters. Serve with papaya salsa.

Nutrition facts per serving: 321 cal., 12 g total fat (6 g sat. fat), 25 mg chol., 333 mg sodium, 38 g carb., 17 g protein.

gazpacho SANGWICHES

This hearty sandwich features the flavors of the chilled Spanish soup called gazpacho. For the filling, grilled tomatoes and onions are stirred together with cucumbers, jalapeño chile peppers, and black beans. The mixture is scooped into grilled bread "bowls."

Prep: 20 minutes
Grill: 12 minutes
Makes: 6 servings

1 medium cucumber, seeded and chopped

1 cup cooked or canned black beans, rinsed and drained

¼ cup snipped fresh cilantro

2 tablespoons cider vinegar

1 tablespoon olive oil

1 pickled jalapeño chile pepper, finely chopped (see tip, page 8)

½ to 1 teaspoon chili powder

1 clove garlic, minced

Salt and ground black pepper

3 large tomatoes, halved

1 large sweet onion (such as Vidalia, Maui, Texas Sweet, or Walla Walla), sliced ½ inch thick

1 loaf French bread

1 In a medium bowl, combine cucumber, beans, cilantro, vinegar, oil, jalapeño pepper, chili powder, and garlic. Season to taste with salt and black pepper. Set aside.

2 Place the tomatoes and onion slices on the lightly greased rack of an grill directly over medium coals. Grill for 12 to 15 minutes or until lightly charred, turning onion slices once. Transfer vegetables to a cutting board; cool slightly and coarsely chop. Add chopped vegetables to the cucumber mixture; toss to combine.

3 Meanwhile, halve the French bread lengthwise. Cut each bread half crosswise into 3 pieces. Using a fork, hollow out the bread pieces slightly. Place the bread pieces, cut sides down, on the rack of the grill directly over medium coals. Grill for about 1 minute or until toasted. Spoon the bean mixture into the bread "bowls."

Nutrition facts per serving: 295 cal., 5 g total fat (1 g sat. fat), 0 mg chol., 671 mg sodium, 54 g carb., 11 g protein.

82

beef
& PORK

Caliente Pot Roast, *page 96*

beef TACO HASH

Start to Finish: 30 minutes
Makes: 4 servings

1 **pound lean ground beef or pork**

2 **tablespoons vegetable oil**

3 **cups frozen diced hash brown potatoes with onions and peppers (½ of a 28-ounce package)**

1 **16-ounce jar chipotle salsa or desired salsa (1¾ cups)**

1 **11-ounce can whole kernel corn with sweet peppers, drained**

1 **cup shredded Mexican-style four-cheese blend (4 ounces)**

2 **cups shredded lettuce**

1 **cup chopped tomatoes (2 medium)**

Sour cream

1 In a large skillet, cook meat over medium-high heat until brown; transfer to a colander to drain off fat.

2 In the same skillet, heat oil over medium heat. Add hash browns, spreading in an even layer. Cook, without stirring, for 6 minutes. Stir potatoes; spread in an even layer. Cook, without stirring, for 3 to 4 minutes more or until brown.

3 Stir in meat, salsa, and corn; heat through. Sprinkle with cheese. Sprinkle with lettuce and tomato. Top with sour cream. Serve from skillet.

Nutrition facts per serving: 614 cal., 36 g total fat (14 g sat. fat), 108 mg chol., 1313 mg sodium, 43 g carb., 33 g protein.

guadalupe BEEF PIE

Prep: 30 minutes
Bake: 30 minutes
Oven: 375°F
Makes: 8 to 10 servings

2¼ cups packaged biscuit mix

½ cup cold water

1 pound ground beef

1 8-ounce carton
  sour cream

1 cup shredded cheddar
  cheese (4 ounces)

⅔ cup mayonnaise

2 tablespoons
  chopped onion

2 medium tomatoes,
  thinly sliced

1 medium green sweet
  pepper, chopped (¾ cup)

  Pimiento-stuffed green
  olives, halved (optional)

1 Preheat oven to 375°F. Grease a 3-quart rectangular baking dish. For crust, in a medium bowl combine biscuit mix and cold water, stirring with a fork until biscuit mix is moistened and a soft dough has formed. Press mixture onto the bottom and ½ inch up the sides of the prepared baking dish. Bake, uncovered, for about 12 minutes or until lightly browned.

2 Meanwhile, in a large skillet, cook ground meat over medium heat until brown. Drain off fat. In a medium bowl, combine sour cream, cheese, mayonnaise, and onion.

3 Sprinkle cooked meat over baked crust. Layer tomatoes over meat and sprinkle with sweet pepper. Spread sour cream mixture over ingredients in dish.

4 Bake, uncovered, for about 30 minutes or until bubbly around edges. If desired, top with olives.

Nutrition facts per serving: 516 cal., 43 g total fat (15 g sat. fat), 75 mg chol., 653 mg sodium, 26 g carb., 17 g protein.

deep-dish MEXICAN MEAT LOAF PIE

Prep: 40 minutes
Bake: 1 hour
Cool: 15 minutes
Oven: 350°F
Makes: 6 servings

1¼ pounds ground beef
(90% lean)

1 cup finely crushed tortilla
chips or corn chips

1 envelope onion soup mix
(½ of a 2-ounce package)

¾ cup bottled taco sauce

2 eggs, lightly beaten
(divided)

1 8.8-ounce pouch cooked
Spanish-style rice (such as
Uncle Ben's Ready Rice)

1 15.5-ounce can golden
hominy, rinsed
and drained

1 14.5-ounce can diced
tomatoes with green
chiles, drained

1 cup shredded pepper Jack
cheese (4 ounces)

1 medium fresh Anaheim
chile pepper, seeded and
chopped (½ cup)

¼ cup chopped
fresh cilantro

Tortilla or corn chips,
sliced fresh jalapeño
chile pepper (see tip,
page 8), and/or fresh
cilantro sprigs

1 Preheat oven to 350°F. Combine beef, crushed chips, soup mix, ½ cup of the taco sauce, 1 lightly beaten egg, and ½ teaspoon black pepper. Press mixture into the bottom and up the sides of a 10-inch deep-dish pie plate.

2 Heat rice according to package directions. In a large bowl, combine rice, hominy, tomatoes, cheese, Anaheim pepper, chopped cilantro, remaining ¼ cup taco sauce, and remaining egg. Spoon mixture into meat shell. Place pie plate on a baking sheet. Cover loosely with foil.

3 Bake for 40 minutes. Remove foil and bake for 20 minutes more or until an instant-read thermometer registers 160°F. Let cool for 15 minutes. Top with chips, jalapeño, and cilantro sprigs.

Nutrition facts per serving: 493 cal., 21 g total fat (8 g sat. fat), 150 mg chol., 1355 mg sodium, 41 g carb., 29 g protein.

mexican beef bake WITH CILANTRO-LIME CREAM

Prep: 25 minutes
Bake: 33 minutes
Oven: 350°F
Makes: 6 servings

- **4 ounces dried multigrain or regular rotini or elbow macaroni (1⅓ cups)**
- **12 ounces extra-lean ground beef**
- **2 cloves garlic, minced**
- **1 15-ounce can black beans or pinto beans, rinsed and drained**
- **1 14.5-ounce can no-salt-added diced tomatoes, undrained**
- **¾ cup bottled picante sauce or salsa**
- **1 teaspoon dried oregano, crushed**
- **½ teaspoon ground cumin**
- **½ teaspoon chili powder**
- **½ cup shredded reduced-fat Co-Jack cheese blend (2 ounces)**
- **⅓ cup light sour cream**
- **3 tablespoons sliced scallions**
- **2 teaspoons coarsely chopped fresh cilantro**
- **½ teaspoon finely shredded lime zest**

1 Preheat oven to 350°F. In a large saucepan, cook pasta according to package directions; drain. Return pasta to hot saucepan; set aside.

2 Meanwhile, in a large skillet, cook meat and garlic until meat is brown, stirring to break up meat as it cooks. Drain off fat.

3 Stir the cooked meat into pasta in saucepan. Stir in beans, tomatoes, picante sauce, oregano, cumin, and chili powder. Transfer mixture to a 1½- to 2-quart casserole or baking dish.

4 Bake, covered, for about 30 minutes or until heated through. Uncover and sprinkle with cheese. Bake, uncovered, for about 3 minutes more or until cheese is melted.

5 In a small bowl, stir together sour cream, 2 tablespoons of the scallions, the cilantro, and lime zest. To serve, top each serving with a spoonful of the sour cream mixture. Sprinkle with the remaining scallions.

Nutrition facts per serving: 283 cal., 10 g total fat (4 g sat. fat), 45 mg chol., 520 mg sodium, 29 g carb., 23 g protein.

mexican PIZZAS

Prep: 10 minutes
Bake: 16 minutes
Cook: 8 minutes
Oven: 425°F
Makes: 12 pizzas

12 **6-inch corn tortillas**
    Nonstick cooking spray
 1 **pound ground beef sirloin**
 1 **green sweet pepper,**
    seeded and sliced into
    thin strips
 1 **red sweet pepper, seeded**
    and sliced into thin strips
 1 **1.25-ounce packet taco**
    seasoning
1½ **cups canned refried beans**
    or bean dip
1½ **cups shredded taco-blend**
    cheese (6 ounces)
    Lime wedges
    Sour cream

1 Preheat oven to 425°F. Place tortillas, overlapping slightly, on two baking sheets. Coat with nonstick cooking spray; flip over and coat bottoms. Bake for 7 minutes. Flip tortillas over; rotate pans. Bake for about 7 minutes longer or until crisp and lightly browned.

2 In a large nonstick skillet, brown ground sirloin for 4 minutes, breaking up clumps. Stir in pepper strips and taco seasoning; cook for 4 minutes.

3 Spread each tortilla with 2 tablespoons of the refried beans. Top each with heaping ¼ cup of the meat mixture and 2 tablespoons of the cheese. Bake for 2 minutes to melt cheese. Serve with lime wedges and sour cream on the side.

Nutrition facts per pizza: 260 cal., 13 g total fat (6 g sat. fat), 53 mg chol., 584 mg sodium, 18 g carb., 17 g protein.

mexican biscuit CASSEROLE

If you like, serve tortilla chips alongside to dip into this taco-flavored hot dish.

Prep: 20 minutes
Bake: 20 minutes
Stand: 5 minutes
Oven: 350°F
Makes: 8 to 10 servings

1½ **pounds lean ground beef**

1 **1.25-ounce package taco seasoning mix**

¾ **cup water**

1 **16-ounce can kidney beans**

1 **11-ounce can whole kernel corn with sweet peppers, drained**

3¼ **cups packaged biscuit mix**

1 **cup milk**

3 **cups shredded cheddar cheese (12 ounces)**

1 Preheat oven to 350°F. In a large skillet, cook ground beef until brown. Drain off fat. Add taco seasoning mix and the ¾ cup water. Add the undrained kidney beans and the drained corn; bring to boiling.

2 Meanwhile, combine the biscuit mix and milk. Stir until all is moistened. Beat for 30 seconds more. Roll dough out on a lightly floured surface to ½-inch thickness. Cut with a 2-inch round biscuit cutter, making 10 biscuits.

3 Spoon hot meat mixture into a 3-quart rectangular baking dish and top with some of the cheese. Immediately place biscuits on top and bake for 20 minutes or until biscuits are tender. Sprinkle with remaining cheese. Let stand for 5 minutes.

Nutrition facts per serving: 486 cal., 25 g total fat (11 g sat. fat), 81 mg chol., 1365 mg sodium, 40 g carb., 29 g protein.

caliente POT ROAST

Caliente means "hot to the touch" in Spanish. The fiery Tex-Mex influence is the ultimate complement to this succulent beef pot roast. Avocado and sour cream offer a creamy, cooling counterpart to the picante sauce.

Start to Finish: 25 minutes
Makes: 4 to 6 servings

- 1 **17-ounce package refrigerated cooked beef roast au jus**
- 1½ **cups packaged sliced fresh mushrooms**
- 1 **cup picante sauce**
- 1 **14-ounce can chicken broth**
- 1 **cup quick-cooking couscous**
- 2 **tablespoons snipped fresh cilantro**
  Sour cream (optional)
  Chopped fresh tomato (optional)
  Sliced avocado (optional)

1 Transfer liquid from roast package to a large skillet; add mushrooms and picante sauce. Cut roast into 1- to 1½-inch pieces; add to skillet. Bring to boiling; reduce heat. Simmer, covered, for 10 minutes.

2 Meanwhile, in a medium saucepan bring broth to boiling; stir in couscous. Cover and remove from heat. Let stand for about 5 minutes or until liquid is absorbed. Fluff with a fork; stir in cilantro.

3 Spoon meat mixture over hot cooked couscous mixture. If desired, serve with sour cream, tomato, and avocado.

Nutrition facts per serving: 370 cal., 9 g total fat (3 g sat. fat), 61 mg chol., 1268 mg sodium, 44 g carb., 31 g protein.

roast beef TAMALE CASSEROLE

A mild poblano chile pepper provides a hint of heat in this modern dish. When buying, look for peppers that are firm and dark green.

Prep: 30 minutes
Bake: 25 minutes
Oven: 350°F
Makes: 4 to 6 servings

1 **17-ounce package refrigerated cooked beef roast au jus**

1 **medium fresh poblano or Anaheim chile pepper, seeded and sliced (see tip, page 8)**

1 **medium onion, chopped**

2 **tablespoon butter**

2 **tablespoons all-purpose flour**

1 **15-ounce can pinto beans, rinsed and drained**

1½ **cups 1-inch pieces zucchini and/or yellow summer squash**

1 **cup grape tomatoes, halved if desired**

¾ **of a 16-ounce tube refrigerated cooked polenta, cut into ½-inch slices**

4 **ounces Monterey Jack cheese with jalapeño chile peppers, shredded (1 cup)**

½ **cup sour cream**

1 **tablespoon snipped fresh cilantro**

Lime wedges

1 Preheat oven to 350°F. Heat beef according to package directions. Pour juice into 2-cup glass measure; add water to equal 1 cup. Coarsely shred beef with two forks.

2 In a large skillet, cook pepper and onion in hot butter over medium heat until tender. Stir in flour. Add juice mixture; cook until thickened and bubbly. Stir in beef, beans, zucchini, and tomatoes. Transfer to lightly greased 2-quart (8×8×2-inch) baking dish. Arrange polenta slices around edges.

3 Bake, uncovered, for 20 minutes. Sprinkle with cheese. Bake for 5 to 10 minutes more, until cheese is melted. Let stand for 5 minutes.

4 In a small bowl, combine sour cream and cilantro. Serve with casserole, and pass lime wedges.

Nutrition facts per serving: 578 cal., 31 g total fat (18 g sat. fat), 125 mg chol., 1155 mg sodium, 40 g carb., 41 g protein.

shredded beef AND CHILE ENCHILADAS

Prep: 35 minutes
Roast: 3 hours
Stand: 15 minutes
Bake: 40 minutes
Oven: 325°F/350°F
Makes: 12 enchiladas

- 1 **3-pound fresh beef brisket**
- 4½ **teaspoons chili powder**
- 1 **tablespoon ground cumin**
- 1 **teaspoon dried oregano, crushed**
- 2 **medium onions, thinly sliced**
- 1 **14-ounce can beef broth**
- ¼ **cup white wine vinegar**
- 2 **4-ounce cans diced green chile peppers**
- 1 **tablespoon all-purpose flour**
- 1 **8-ounce carton sour cream**
- 2 **cups shredded Monterey Jack cheese (8 ounces)**
- 12 **7- to 8-inch flour tortillas**
- 1 **cup salsa verde or desired salsa**

1 Preheat oven to 325°F. Trim fat from brisket. In a small bowl, combine 4 teaspoons of the chili powder, the cumin, and oregano. Sprinkle spice mixture evenly over all sides of the brisket; rub in with your fingers.

2 Place brisket in a shallow roasting pan. Top with sliced onions and pour broth and vinegar over meat. Roast, covered, for about 3 hours or until meat is fork-tender. Let meat stand in pan juices for about 15 minutes or until cool enough to handle. Remove meat from pan. Using a slotted spoon, remove onions; reserve pan juices. Halve meat crosswise. Using two forks, pull meat apart into shreds. Stir onions into shredded meat; stir in enough of the reserved pan juices to moisten (½ to 1 cup). Set meat mixture aside. Discard remaining pan juices.

3 In a medium saucepan, combine undrained chile peppers and the remaining ½ teaspoon chili powder; cook for about 1 minute or until heated through. Stir in flour. Cook and stir for 1 minute more. Remove from heat. Stir in sour cream and ½ cup of the cheese.

4 Increase oven temperature to 350°F. Grease a 3-quart rectangular baking dish. Divide shredded meat mixture among tortillas. Top with sour cream mixture. Roll up tortillas (tortillas will be full). Arrange rolled tortillas, seam sides down, in prepared baking dish. Bake, covered, for 30 minutes. Uncover. Spoon salsa verde over; sprinkle with the remaining 1½ cups cheese. Bake, uncovered, for about 10 minutes more or until cheese is melted and enchiladas are heated through.

Nutrition facts per enchilada: 559 cal., 38 g total fat (17 g sat. fat), 118 mg chol., 716 mg sodium, 23 g carb., 29 g protein.

steak tacos AL CARBON

Prep: 30 minutes
Marinate: 4 to 24 hours
Grill: 14 minutes
Makes: 12 tacos

2 **pounds beef skirt steak**
½ **cup lime juice**
2 **tablespoons vegetable oil**
2 **teaspoons chili powder**
4 **cloves garlic, minced**
1 **teaspoon salt**
12 **scallions, or 2 medium onions, cut into 12 slices total**
1 **teaspoon vegetable oil**
12 **8-inch flour tortillas**
  Refrigerated guacamole
  Chipotle salsa, other salsa, or pico de gallo
  Snipped fresh cilantro

1 Trim fat from meat. Place meat in a large resealable plastic bag. For marinade, in a small bowl combine lime juice, the 2 tablespoons oil, the chili powder, garlic, and salt. Pour marinade over meat. Seal bag; turn to coat meat. Marinate in the refrigerator for 4 to 24 hours, turning bag occasionally.

2 Trim scallions, if using. Brush onions with the 1 teaspoon oil. Stack tortillas and wrap in foil.

3 For a charcoal grill, place onions and tortilla packet on the rack of an uncovered grill directly over medium-hot coals. (Be sure to lay scallions perpendicular to the grill grates so they won't fall into the coals.) Grill just until onions are tender and tortillas are warm, turning occasionally. Allow 4 to 5 minutes for the onions and about 10 minutes for the tortillas. (For a gas grill, preheat grill. Reduce heat to medium-high. Place onions and tortilla packet on grill rack over heat. Cover and grill as above.) Transfer onions to a bowl; cover with foil to keep warm. Remove tortillas from grill.

4 Drain meat, discarding marinade. Grill meat on rack directly over medium-high heat for about 4 minutes or until slightly pink in center, turning once halfway through grilling. Remove from grill. Slice meat diagonally across the grain into 1½-inch-wide strips. If desired, cut the onions into 1-inch pieces.

5 Fill warm tortillas with meat and onions. Serve with guacamole, chipotle salsa, and cilantro.

Nutrition facts per taco: 354 cal., 17 g total fat (5 g sat. fat), 45 mg chol., 588 mg sodium, 29 g carb., 21 g protein.

grilled STEAK FAJITAS

Prep: 25 minutes
Grill: 20 minutes
Makes: 4 servings

- 3 green and/or red sweet peppers, sliced
- 1 medium onion, sliced
- 1 tablespoon olive oil
- 1½ teaspoons fajita seasoning
- 1 clove garlic, minced
- 1 pound boneless beef top sirloin steak, cut 1 inch thick
- 4 8-inch whole wheat tortillas
  Purchased salsa (optional)
  Sour cream (optional)

1 Fold a 36×18-inch piece of heavy foil in half crosswise. Place sweet peppers and onion in the center of the foil. Drizzle with oil; sprinkle with ½ teaspoon of the fajita seasoning and the garlic. Bring up the opposite edges of the foil; seal with a double fold. Fold in remaining edges, leaving space for steam to build. Set aside.

2 Sprinkle the remaining 1 teaspoon fajita seasoning on both sides of steak; rub in with your fingers. For a charcoal grill, place steak and the vegetable packet on the rack of an uncovered grill directly over medium coals. Grill steak until desired doneness, turning once halfway through grilling. Allow 14 to 18 minutes for medium-rare doneness (145°F) or 18 to 22 minutes for medium doneness (160°F). Remove steak and keep warm. Grill vegetables for about 20 minutes or until tender. (For a gas grill, preheat grill. Reduce heat to medium. Place steak and vegetable packet on grill rack over heat. Cover and grill as above.)

3 Meanwhile, wrap tortillas in foil. Place tortilla packet next to steak on grill rack; grill for about 10 minutes or until tortillas are heated through. Slice meat into thin bite-size strips. Divide meat among tortillas; top with vegetables. Roll up. If desired, serve with salsa and sour cream.

Nutrition facts per serving: 333 cal., 12 g total fat (3 g sat. fat), 69 mg chol., 454 mg sodium, 22 g carb., 33 g protein.

beef AND CHIPOTLE BURRITOS

Chipotle peppers are smoked jalapeños that lend a great smoky flavor to foods. Find them at the supermarket next to the canned chile peppers.

Prep: 20 minutes
Cook: 8 to 10 hours (low)
or 4 to 5 hours
(high)
Makes: 6 servings

1½ **pounds boneless beef round steak, cut ¾ inch thick**

1 **14.5-ounce can diced tomatoes, undrained**

⅓ **cup chopped onion (1 small)**

1 **to 2 canned chipotle chile peppers in adobo sauce, chopped (see tip, page 8)**

1 **teaspoon dried oregano, crushed**

¼ **teaspoon ground cumin**

1 **clove garlic, minced**

6 **9- to 10-inch tomato-flavored or plain flour tortillas, warmed**

¾ **cup shredded sharp cheddar cheese (3 ounces)**

Pico de Gallo Salsa*

Shredded jicama or radishes (optional)

Sour cream (optional)

1 Trim fat from meat. Cut meat into 6 pieces. In a 3½- or 4-quart slow cooker, place meat, tomatoes, onion, chipotle peppers, oregano, cumin, and garlic.

2 Cover and cook on low-heat setting for 8 to 10 hours or on high-heat setting for 4 to 5 hours. Remove meat from cooker. Using two forks, pull meat apart into shreds. Place meat in a large bowl. Stir in enough cooking liquid to reach desired consistency. Divide meat among warm tortillas, spooning it just below the centers. Top with cheese, Pico de Gallo Salsa, and, if desired, jicama and sour cream. Roll up tortillas.

***Pico de Gallo Salsa:** In a medium bowl, combine 2 finely chopped medium tomatoes; 2 tablespoons finely chopped onion; 2 tablespoons snipped fresh cilantro; 1 fresh serrano chile pepper, seeded and finely chopped (see tip, page 8); and pinch of sugar. Cover; chill for several hours.

Nutrition facts per serving: 361 cal., 13 g total fat (5 g sat. fat), 71 mg chol., 433 mg sodium, 29 g carb., 30 g protein.

ancho-rubbed PRIME RIB STEAKS WITH GRILLED-MANGO BUTTER

Ancho chile peppers are the dried version of the mildly spicy poblano, a dark green pepper slightly smaller than a bell pepper.

Prep: 30 minutes
Grill: 30 minutes
Makes: 10 servings

2   **2-pound beef rib steaks, cut 2 to 2½ inches thick**

2   **tablespoons ground ancho chile pepper**

1   **tablespoon unsweetened cocoa powder**

½   **teaspoon kosher salt**

½   **teaspoon ground black pepper**

1   **tablespoon olive oil**
    Grilled-Mango Butter*

1 Trim fat from steaks. For rub, in a small bowl, combine ancho chile pepper, cocoa powder, salt, and black pepper. Brush steaks with oil. Sprinkle pepper mixture evenly over steaks; rub in with your gloved fingers.

2 For a charcoal grill, arrange medium-hot coals around a drip pan. Test for medium heat above pan. Place steaks on grill rack over drip pan. Cover and grill for 30 to 35 minutes for medium-rare (145°F) or 35 to 40 minutes for medium (160°F). (For a gas gill, preheat grill. Reduce heat to medium. Adjust for indirect cooking. Grill as above.)

3 Cut steaks into serving-size pieces. Serve with Grilled-Mango Butter.

***Grilled-Mango Butter:** Seed and peel 1 small mango; cut mango into ¼-inch slices. Lightly brush slices with olive oil. For a charcoal grill, grill mango on the rack of an uncovered grill directly over medium-hot coals for 5 minutes, turning once. (For a gas grill, preheat grill. Reduce heat to medium-high. Place mango on grill rack over heat. Cover and grill as directed.) Chop the grilled mango. In a food processor, combine the chopped mango and ¾ cup butter, softened. Cover and process with several on/off pulses until mango is finely chopped.

Nutrition facts per serving: 574 cal., 49 g total fat (23 g sat. fat), 141 mg chol., 267 mg sodium, 6 g carb., 27 g protein.

chiles en nogada
(CHILES IN WALNUT SAUCE)

Prep: 45 minutes
Bake: 20 minutes
Oven: 425°F/350°F
Makes: 8 servings

- 8 large fresh poblano chile peppers (see tip, page 8)
- 12 ounces ground pork
- ½ cup chopped onion (1 medium)
- 1 medium fresh jalapeño chile pepper, seeded and finely chopped (see tip, page 8; optional)
- 1 clove garlic, minced Vegetable oil (optional)
- 1 8-ounce can whole kernel corn, drained
- 2 large tomatoes, peeled, seeded, and chopped (about 1⅓ cups)
- 1 large pear, cored and coarsely shredded (about 1 cup)
- ¼ cup raisins
- ½ teaspoon salt
- ¼ teaspoon ground cinnamon
- ¼ teaspoon ground black pepper
- ½ cup pecans or pine nuts, toasted
- 1 8-ounce carton sour cream
- 2 tablespoons milk
- 1 teaspoon lime juice
- ⅛ teaspoon ground cinnamon Toasted pumpkin seeds (pepitas)

1 Preheat oven to 425°F. Place whole poblano peppers on a foil-lined baking sheet. Bake for 15 to 20 minutes or until skins are charred and blistered, turning once or twice. Bring foil up around peppers to enclose. Let stand about 15 minutes or until cool enough to handle. With gloved hands, use a paring knife to peel skins away from peppers. Carefully cut one vertical slit down each poblano pepper (the whole length of the pepper), keeping stem intact. Remove seeds. Reduce oven temperature to 350°F.

2 Meanwhile, for picadillo, in a large skillet cook ground pork, onion, jalapeño pepper (if desired), and garlic until meat is no longer pink. Add oil, if needed, to prevent sticking. Drain off fat. Stir corn, tomatoes, pear, raisins, salt, the ¼ teaspoon cinnamon, and the black pepper into meat mixture. Reduce heat. Simmer, uncovered, for 10 minutes. Cool.

3 Spoon about ½ cup of the picadillo into each pepper. Place peppers in a 3-quart rectangular baking dish. Bake, uncovered, in the 350°F oven for about 20 minutes or until heated through.

4 Meanwhile, for nut sauce, place nuts in a blender or food processor. Cover and blend or process until finely ground. In a small bowl, stir together nuts, sour cream, milk, lime juice, and the ⅛ teaspoon cinnamon. To serve, top peppers with nut sauce and pumpkin seeds.

Nutrition facts per serving: 330 cal., 20 g total fat (7 g sat. fat), 46 mg chol., 287 mg sodium, 27 g carb., 12 g protein.

tamale PIE

Prep: 35 minutes
Cook: 10 minutes
Bake: 30 minutes
Oven: 350°F
Makes: 6 servings

1⅓ **cups water**

½ **cup yellow cornmeal**

½ **cup cold water**

½ **teaspoon salt**

8 **ounces ground pork**

½ **cup chopped green
and/or red sweet pepper**

1 **tablespoon chili powder**

1 **14.5-ounce can diced
tomatoes with onion
and garlic, drained**

1 **11-ounce can whole
kernel corn, drained**

2 **tablespoons tomato paste**

½ **cup shredded reduced-fat
cheddar cheese (2 ounces)**

2 **tablespoons snipped
fresh cilantro**

1 Preheat oven to 350°F. Lightly coat a 2-quart square baking dish with nonstick cooking spray. In a small saucepan, bring the 1⅓ cups water to boiling. Meanwhile, in a small bowl stir together cornmeal, the ½ cup cold water, and ¼ teaspoon of the salt. Slowly add the cornmeal mixture to the boiling water, stirring constantly. Cook and stir until mixture returns to boiling; reduce heat. Cook over low heat for about 10 minutes or until mixture is very thick, stirring frequently.

2 Spoon the hot cornmeal mixture into the prepared baking dish. Cover and chill while preparing filling.

3 For filling, in a large skillet cook pork and sweet pepper until meat is brown. Drain off fat. Stir chili powder and the remaining ¼ teaspoon salt into meat mixture in skillet; cook for 1 minute. Stir in the tomatoes, corn, and tomato paste. Spoon the meat mixture on the chilled cornmeal mixture in the baking dish.

4 Bake, uncovered, for about 30 minutes or until heated through. Sprinkle with cheese and cilantro.

Nutrition facts per serving: 246 cal., 11 g total fat (4 g sat. fat), 34 mg chol., 812 mg sodium, 26 g carb., 12 g protein.

southwest PORK CHOPS

Prep: 15 minutes
Cook: 5 hours (low) or
    2½ hours (high)
Makes: 6 servings

6 **pork rib chops, cut ¾ inch thick (about 2½ pounds)**

1 **15-ounce can Mexican-style or Tex-Mex-style chili beans**

1¼ **cups bottled salsa**

1 **cup fresh* or frozen whole kernel corn**

2 **cups hot cooked rice**

Snipped fresh cilantro (optional)

Trim excess fat from chops. Place chops in the bottom of a 3½- or 4-quart slow cooker. Add chili beans and salsa. Cover; cook on high-heat setting for 2½ hours or low-heat setting for 5 hours. When that step is complete, turn to high-heat setting, if necessary. Stir in corn. Cover and cook for 30 minutes longer. Serve over rice. Sprinkle with cilantro, if desired.

Nutrition facts per serving: 334 cal., 7 g total fat (2 g sat. fat), 77 mg chol., 716 mg sodium, 34 g carb., 33 g protein.

For all-day cooking: Substitute 8 boneless pork chops for the 6 rib chops. (When cooked this long, chops with bone may leave bony fragments in the cooked mixture.) Cover and cook on low-heat setting for 9½ hours. Turn to high-heat setting. Stir in corn. Cover and cook for 30 minutes longer. Serve as above.

*Tip: Two medium ears of fresh corn equal about 1 cup of whole kernel corn.

pork tenderloin WITH
RED MOLE

Prep: 30 minutes
Stand: 40 minutes
Cook: 30 minutes
Grill: 30 minutes
Makes: 8 to 10 servings

- **2 dried ancho chile peppers (see tip, page 8)**
- **½ cup diced white onion**
- **2 cloves garlic, smashed**
- **2 tablespoons cooking oil**
- **½ cup raw sunflower kernels**
- **½ teaspoon ground cinnamon**
- **½ teaspoon cumin seeds**
- **⅛ teaspoon allspice**
- **2½ cups chicken broth**
- **1 large tomato, peeled, seeded, and chopped**
- **2 slices firm white bread, torn into pieces**
- **2 canned chipotle chile peppers in adobo sauce**
- **½ ounce semisweet chocolate, chopped**
- **2 teaspoons sugar**
- **Salt and ground black pepper**
- **Sugar**
- **2 1- to 1½-pound pork tenderloins**
- **Pumpkin seeds (pepitas), toasted**

1 In a large dry skillet, toast ancho peppers on both sides until they crackle and just turn color, about 1 minute on each side. (Be careful not to burn them; it will make your mole bitter.) Place in a small bowl; cover with boiling water and let stand for 30 minutes to rehydrate. Drain and discard soaking water. Remove seeds from ancho peppers; set aside.

2 In the same large skillet, cook onion and garlic in hot oil over medium heat for 5 minutes or until onion is tender. Stir in sunflower kernels, cinnamon, cumin seeds, and allspice; cook and stir for 3 to 4 minutes more or until mixture is very fragrant. Transfer mixture to a blender or food processor.

3 Add 1½ cups of the chicken broth, the tomato, bread, ancho peppers, and chipotle peppers to the blender or food processor. Cover and blend or process until smooth, adding more chicken broth if needed.

4 Transfer mixture to a large saucepan. Stir in remaining broth, chocolate, and 2 teaspoons sugar. Bring mixture to boiling; reduce heat and simmer, uncovered, for 30 minutes or until mixture reaches desired consistency. Season to taste with salt, pepper, and additional sugar. Cover and keep warm.

5 Meanwhile, season pork tenderloins with salt and black pepper. For a charcoal grill, arrange hot coals around a drip pan. Test for medium-high heat above pan. Place meat on grill rack over pan. Cover; grill for 30 to 35 minutes or until a meat thermometer registers 155°F. (For a gas grill, preheat grill. Reduce heat to medium. Adjust for indirect cooking. Grill as above.) Remove meat from grill. Cover with foil and let stand for 10 minutes. (The meat's temperature will rise 5°F during standing.) Slice tenderloin into ½-inch-thick slices.

6 Place tenderloin slices on a serving plate. Top with mole sauce and sprinkle with pumpkin seeds.

Nutrition facts per serving: 282 cal., 14 g total fat (2 g sat. fat), 74 mg chol., 498 mg sodium, 13 g carb., 28 g protein.

lime jerk PORK WITH SALSA

Prep: 30 minutes
Marinate: 1 hour
Grill: 30 minutes
Makes: 8 servings

- **2 tablespoon finely shredded lime zest**
- **⅓ cup lime juice**
- **2 tablespoon packed brown sugar**
- **1 tablespoon canola oil**
- **1 tablespoon Jamaican jerk seasoning**
- **2 cloves garlic, minced**
- **¼ teaspoon cayenne pepper**
- **2 pork tenderloins (about ¾ pound each)**
- **Salsa***

1 For marinade, in a bowl combine all ingredients except pork and Salsa. Place pork in a large self-sealing plastic bag set in a shallow dish. Pour marinade over pork. Seal bag. Marinate in refrigerator for 1 hour; turn bag occasionally. Drain pork; discard marinade.

2 For a charcoal grill, arrange hot coals around a drip pan. Test for medium-hot heat above pan. Place meat on grill rack over the drip pan. Cover and grill for 30 to 35 minutes or until an instant-read thermometer inserted in meat registers 155°F. (For a gas grill, preheat grill. Reduce heat to medium-high. Adjust for indirect cooking. Place meat on rack in a roasting pan, place on grill rack, and grill as above.) Let stand for 10 minutes. Slice tenderloins and serve with Salsa.

*****Salsa:** In a small bowl, combine 1 cup chopped banana; ⅓ cup raisins; 2 medium fresh jalapeño chile peppers, seeded and finely chopped (see tip, page 8); 3 tablespoons lime juice; 2 tablespoons finely chopped red onion; 1 tablespoon canola oil; 1 tablespoon frozen orange juice concentrate, thawed; 2 teaspoons snipped fresh cilantro; 1 teaspoon ground coriander; 1 teaspoon honey; and 1 teaspoon grated fresh ginger. Makes 1½ cups.

Nutrition facts per serving: 167 cal., 5 g total fat (1 g sat. fat), 55 mg chol., 64 mg sodium, 13 g carb., 18 g protein.

shredded SAVORY PORK TACOS

Like tacos but ready for more zing? Try this version. Boneless pork loin blade roast is a tender, moist meat that simmers into a shredded taco base seasoned with aromatic and flavorful coriander, cumin, and oregano. The pork's got plenty of flavor—let your salsa deliver the spiciness as you like it.

Prep: 25 minutes
Cook: 8 to 10 hours (low)
    or 4 to 5 hours
    (high)
Makes: 6 (2-taco) servings

1 2- to 2½-pound boneless
   pork loin blade roast

2 large onions, quartered
   (2 cups)

3 fresh jalapeño chile
   peppers, seeded if
   desired, and cut up (see
   tip, page 8)

8 cloves garlic, minced

2 teaspoons ground
   coriander

2 teaspoons ground cumin

2 teaspoons dried
   oregano, crushed

½ teaspoon salt

½ teaspoon ground black
   pepper

1 cup water

12 6-inch flour tortillas,
   warmed according to
   package directions

Salsa (optional)

Sour cream (optional)

Shredded cheddar cheese
(optional)

Guacamole (optional)

Lime wedges (optional)

1 Trim fat from meat. Place meat in a 3½- or 4-quart slow cooker. Add onions, jalapeño peppers, garlic, coriander, cumin, oregano, salt, and black pepper to cooker. Pour the water over mixture in cooker.

2 Cover and cook on low-heat setting for 8 to 10 hours or on high-heat setting for 4 to 5 hours.

3 Remove meat from cooker with a slotted spoon; discard remaining cooking liquid and solids. When cool enough to handle, shred meat by pulling through it with two forks in opposite directions. To serve, fill each tortilla with meat. If desired, top individual servings with salsa, sour cream, cheese, guacamole, and/or lime wedges.

Nutrition facts per serving: 388 cal., 18 g total fat (5 g sat. fat), 96 mg chol., 396 mg sodium, 24 g carb., 32 g protein.

Make-Ahead Directions: Place shredded meat in a freezer container. Cover and freeze for up to 3 months. Thaw overnight in the refrigerator before using.

tacos AL PASTOR

Prep: 45 minutes
Stand: 30 minutes
Marinate: 4 to 24 hours
Grill: 10 minutes
Makes: 8 to 10 servings

1 medium peeled and cored
   fresh pineapple

8 dried pasilla and/or
   guajillo chile peppers
   (see tip, page 8)

¼ cup orange juice

¼ cup vinegar

4 cloves garlic, minced

½ teaspoon salt

½ teaspoon ground cumin

⅛ teaspoon ground cloves

2 pounds boneless pork loin,
   cut into ½-inch slices

16 6-inch corn tortillas

1 cup chopped onion
   (1 large)

   Snipped fresh cilantro

   Lime wedges

   Bottled hot pepper sauce
   (optional)

1 Cut pineapple into ½-inch-thick slices, reserving juice; cover and refrigerate pineapple and reserved juice separately.

2 Remove stems and seeds from chile peppers. Place peppers in a medium bowl and add enough boiling water to cover. Allow peppers to stand for about 30 minutes or until soft; drain, discarding water.

3 In a food processor or blender, combine chile peppers, any juice from the pineapple, the orange juice, vinegar, garlic, salt, cumin, and cloves. Cover and process or blend until nearly smooth.

4 In a 3-quart baking dish, arrange pork slices in a single layer, overlapping slices as necessary. Pour chile pepper mixture over pork slices, spreading evenly. Cover and marinate in the refrigerator for 4 to 24 hours. Remove pork from marinade, discarding marinade. Stack tortillas and wrap in foil.

5 For a charcoal grill, place tortilla packet on the rack of an uncovered grill directly over medium coals. Place pork slices and pineapple slices on the grill rack alongside the foil packet directly over medium coals. Grill pork and pineapple slices for 6 to 7 minutes or until pork slices are slightly pink in the center and juices run clear (160°F), turning once. Grill tortilla packet for 10 minutes, turning once. (For a gas grill, preheat grill. Reduce heat to medium. Grill tortilla packet, pork slices, and pineapple as directed above.)

6 Coarsely chop pork and pineapple and combine in a large bowl. Fill warm tortillas with pork and pineapple mixture. Sprinkle each taco with chopped onion and cilantro. Serve with lime wedges and, if desired, hot pepper sauce.

Nutrition facts per serving: 362 cal., 11 g total fat (3 g sat. fat), 76 mg chol., 233 mg sodium, 39 g carb., 29 g protein.

pork CHOPS WITH AVOCADO SALSA

Prep: 10 minutes
Start to Finish: 30 minutes
Makes: 4 servings

4   boneless pork loin chops, ¾ inch thick (about 1 pound total)
1   tablespoon cumin seeds, slightly crushed
½   teaspoon salt
¼   teaspoon ground black pepper
2   cloves garlic, minced
2   tablespoons vegetable oil
1   (4-ounce) can tomatillo salsa or ½ cup salsa verde
1   scallion, coarsely chopped
1   ripe avocado, diced
¼   cup chopped radishes
1   tablespoon chopped cilantro

① Trim fat from chops. Rinse and pat dry. Combine cumin, ¼ teaspoon of the salt, pepper, and garlic. Rub mixture evenly over chops.

② In a large skillet, heat oil over medium-high heat. Add chops and cook 8 to 12 minutes or until pork juices run clear (160°F), turning once.

③ In a food processor, blend tomatillo salsa, scallion, and remaining ¼ teaspoon salt until smooth. Transfer to a bowl and stir in avocado, radishes, and fresh cilantro.

Nutrition facts per serving: 280 cal., 16.5 g total fat (3.5 g sat. fat), 66 mg chol., 526 mg sodium, 7 g carb., 26 g protein.

pulled PORK ENCHILADAS

Prep: 40 minutes
Cook: 10 to 11 hours
(low) or 5 to 6
hours (high)
Bake: 30 minutes
Oven: 400°F
Makes: 6 servings

3½ pounds boneless
pork shoulder

1 14-ounce can
chicken broth

½ cup chopped onion
(1 medium)

6 cloves garlic, minced

1 tablespoon ground cumin

2 to 3 teaspoons ground
chipotle chile pepper or
hot chili powder

1 teaspoon salt

3 10-ounce cans
enchilada sauce

1 tablespoon snipped
fresh cilantro

1 4-ounce can diced green
chile peppers

8 ounces cojita cheese,
shredded (2 cups)

12 8-inch flour tortillas

Snipped fresh cilantro

Diced tomato or quartered
grape tomatoes

Sour cream (optional)

1 Trim fat from pork. In a 3½- or 4-quart slow cooker, combine pork shoulder, broth, onion, garlic, cumin, ground chipotle chile pepper, and salt. Cover and cook on low-heat setting for 10 to 11 hours or on high-heat setting for 5 to 6 hours.

2 Preheat oven to 400°F. Remove pork from slow cooker, reserving cooking liquid. Using two forks, pull meat into coarse strands.

3 In a large bowl, combine pork, ½ cup of the enchilada sauce, 2 tablespoons of the reserved cooking liquid, and the 1 tablespoon snipped cilantro. Set aside.

4 In a medium bowl, combine the remaining enchilada sauce, ¼ cup of the reserved cooking liquid (discard any remaining cooking liquid), and the diced green chile peppers. Spread about ½ cup of enchilada–green chile pepper mixture in the bottom of a 3-quart rectangular baking dish.

5 Divide pork mixture and 1½ cups of the cheese among tortillas, placing meat and cheese near the edge of each tortilla. Roll up tortillas. Place filled tortillas, seam sides down, in the prepared baking dish (place tortillas close together); top with the remaining enchilada–green chile pepper mixture. Cover with foil; bake for 25 minutes. Sprinkle with the remaining ½ cup cheese. Bake, uncovered, about 5 minutes more or until heated through and cheese is softened and starts to brown slightly.

6 Sprinkle with additional snipped cilantro and tomato. If desired, serve with sour cream.

Nutrition facts per serving: 861 cal., 36 g total fat (13 g sat. fat), 212 mg chol., 2795 mg sodium, 64 g carb., 68 g protein.

chile VERDE

Prep: 40 minutes
Cook: 6 to 8 hours (low)
    or 3 to 4 hours
    (high)
Makes: 6 servings

1 teaspoon ground cumin

½ teaspoon salt

¼ teaspoon ground black
   pepper

1½ pounds boneless pork
   shoulder, cut into
   1-inch pieces

1 tablespoon olive oil

1 pound fresh tomatillos,
   husks removed and
   chopped (about 4 cups)

1 cup chopped onion
   (1 large)

3 teaspoons finely shredded
   lime zest

2 tablespoons lime juice

4 cloves garlic, minced

¾ cup chopped yellow or
   red sweet pepper
   (1 medium)

12 6-inch corn tortillas

2 tablespoons snipped
   fresh cilantro

Purchased salsa verde
(optional)

1 In a small bowl, combine cumin, salt, and pepper. Trim fat from meat. Cut meat into 1-inch pieces. Sprinkle cumin mixture over meat. Coat a large skillet with cooking spray. Cook half of the meat in hot skillet over medium heat until brown. Remove meat from skillet. Add oil to skillet. Brown remaining meat in hot oil. Drain off fat. Place meat in a 3½- to 4½-quart slow cooker. Add tomatillos, onion, lime zest, lime juice, and garlic. Stir to combine.

2 Cover and cook on low-heat setting for 6 to 8 hours or on high-heat setting for 3 to 4 hours.

3 If using low-heat setting, turn to high-heat setting. Add sweet pepper to cooker. Cover and cook for 15 minutes more. Fill corn tortillas with meat mixture; sprinkle with cilantro and remaining lime zest. If desired, serve with green salsa.

Nutrition facts per serving: 333 cal., 11 g total fat (3 g sat. fat), 73 mg chol., 314 mg sodium, 32 g carb., 27 g protein.

chiapas-style PORK ROAST

Prep: 30 minutes
Stand: 30 minutes
Chill: 4 to 24 hours
Roast: 2½ hours
Oven: 325°F
Makes: 6 servings

- **3 dried ancho chile peppers, stemmed and seeded (see tip, page 8)**
- **1 3-pound boneless pork shoulder roast**
- **½ cup coarsely chopped onion (1 medium)**
- **½ cup dry sherry**
- **¼ cup cider vinegar**
- **4 cloves garlic**
- **1 teaspoon salt**
- **1 teaspoon paprika**
- **½ teaspoon dried marjoram, crushed**
- **½ teaspoon dried Mexican oregano or dried oregano, crushed**
- **½ teaspoon cracked black pepper**
- **½ teaspoon ground allspice**
- **Coarsely chopped fresh oregano (optional)**

1 In a small bowl, pour enough boiling water over chile peppers to cover; let stand for about 20 minutes or until chile peppers soften. Drain and discard liquid.

2 Meanwhile, trim fat from roast. With the point of a sharp knife, pierce the roast all over, making ½-inch-deep slits. Place roast in a small roasting pan.

3 For the wet rub, in a food processor or blender combine drained chile peppers, onion, sherry, vinegar, garlic, salt, paprika, marjoram, oregano, black pepper, and allspice. Cover and process or blend until nearly smooth.

4 Rub meat generously with the wet rub, making sure to rub it into the slits. Cover roast and chill for 4 to 24 hours.

5 Preheat oven to 325°F. Uncover roast and spoon any of the wet rub in the bottom of the pan over the roast. Cover roasting pan with foil. Roast for 1½ hours. Remove foil. Roast for about 1 hour more or until roast is tender. Let stand for 10 minutes before slicing. Garnish with fresh oregano, if desired.

Nutrition facts per serving: 402 cal., 17 g total fat (6 g sat. fat), 152 mg chol., 566 mg sodium, 9 g carb., 46 g protein.

chicken & TURKEY

Chicken Tostadas, *page 124*

chicken TOSTADAS

This Tex-Mex take on a one-dish meal has everything—bread, chicken, beans, and salad—stacked on one plate. Customize this with your favorite version of salsa.

Prep: 30 minutes
Cook: 5 to 6 hours (low)
or 2½ to 3 hours
(high)
Makes: 10 servings

3 **tablespoons chili powder**

3 **tablespoons lime juice**

2 **fresh jalapeño chile peppers, seeded and finely chopped (see tip, page 8)**

¼ **teaspoon bottled hot pepper sauce**

8 **cloves garlic, minced**

1 **medium onion, sliced and separated into rings**

2 **pounds skinless, boneless chicken thighs**

1 **16-ounce can refried beans**

10 **tostada shells**

1½ **cups shredded cheddar cheese (6 ounces)**

2 **cups shredded lettuce**

1¼ **cups bottled salsa**

¾ **cup sour cream**

¾ **cup sliced pitted black olives (optional)**

1 In a 3½- to 5-quart slow cooker, combine chili powder, lime juice, jalapeño peppers, hot pepper sauce, and garlic. Add onion; place chicken on top of mixture in cooker.

2 Cover and cook on low-heat setting for 5 to 6 hours or on high-heat setting for 2½ to 3 hours.

3 Using a slotted spoon, remove chicken and onion from cooker; reserve ½ cup of the cooking liquid. Shred chicken by pulling two forks through it in opposite directions. In a medium bowl, combine chicken, onion, and the reserved ½ cup cooking liquid.

4 Spread refried beans on tostada shells. Top with chicken mixture and cheese. Serve with lettuce, salsa, sour cream, and, if desired, olives.

Nutrition facts per serving: 333 cal., 16 g total fat (7 g sat. fat), 100 mg chol., 574 mg sodium, 21 g carb., 27 g protein.

spicy chicken AND RICE BAKE

This Mexicali casserole includes black beans and corn. Adjust the cayenne pepper, adding more or less to get the hotness you like.

Prep: 25 minutes
Bake: 55 minutes
Oven: 375°F
Makes: 6 servings

- 1 tablespoon cooking oil
- ½ cup chopped onion (1 medium)
- ½ cup chopped green sweet pepper (1 small)
- 2 cloves garlic, minced
- 1 15-ounce can black beans, rinsed and drained
- 1 14.5-ounce can diced tomatoes, undrained
- 1 cup tomato juice
- 1 cup frozen whole kernel corn
- ⅔ cup long grain rice
- 1 teaspoon chili powder
- ½ teaspoon salt
- ⅛ to ¼ teaspoon cayenne pepper
- 3 pounds meaty chicken pieces (small breast halves, thighs, and drumsticks), skinned
- Salt and ground black pepper
- Paprika

1 Preheat oven to 375°F. In a large saucepan, heat oil over medium heat. Add onion, sweet pepper, and garlic. Cook and stir until vegetables are tender. Stir in black beans, tomatoes, tomato juice, corn, uncooked rice, chili powder, salt, and cayenne. Bring to boiling. Transfer rice mixture to an ungreased 3-quart rectangular baking dish.

2 Arrange chicken pieces on top of the rice mixture. Sprinkle chicken lightly with salt, black pepper, and paprika.

3 Cover tightly with foil. Bake for 55 to 60 minutes or until chicken is no longer pink (170°F for breasts, 180°F for thighs and drumsticks) and rice is tender.

Nutrition facts per serving: 446 cal., 15 g total fat (4 g sat. fat), 104 mg chol., 854 mg sodium, 39 g carb., 40 g protein.

chicken WITH MOLE

Prep: 45 minutes
Stand: 45 minutes
Bake: 35 minutes
Oven: 375°F
Makes: 6 servings

2 dried ancho, mulato, or pasilla chile peppers (see tip, page 8)

1¼ cups chicken broth

1 medium tomato, peeled and cut up

1 medium onion, cut up

⅓ cup slivered almonds, toasted

1 tablespoon sugar

2 cloves garlic, minced

½ ounce unsweetened chocolate, cut up

½ teaspoon ground coriander

¼ teaspoon salt

¼ teaspoon ground cinnamon

2½ to 3 pounds meaty chicken pieces (breasts, thighs, and drumsticks)

1 tablespoon vegetable oil

1 tablespoon sesame seeds, toasted (optional)

1 Cut peppers open; discard stems and seeds. Place peppers in a small bowl and cover with boiling water. Let stand for 45 to 60 minutes to soften; drain well. Cut peppers into small pieces.

2 Preheat oven to 375°F. For mole, in a blender or food processor combine pepper pieces, broth, tomato, onion, almonds, sugar, garlic, chocolate, coriander, salt, and cinnamon. Cover and blend or process until nearly smooth, stopping to scrape side of container, if necessary.

3 Arrange chicken in a lightly greased shallow baking pan. Brush with oil. Bake for 35 to 40 minutes or until chicken is tender and no longer pink (170°F for breasts, 180°F for thighs and drumsticks). Transfer to a serving platter.

4 Meanwhile, transfer mole to a small saucepan. Bring to boiling; reduce heat. Simmer, uncovered, for about 15 minutes or until thickened, stirring frequently. Spoon some of the mole over chicken pieces. If desired, sprinkle with sesame seeds. Pass remaining mole.

Nutrition facts per serving: 314 cal., 18 g total fat (4 g sat. fat), 87 mg chol., 336 mg sodium, 7 g carb., 31 g protein.

Make-Ahead Directions: Prepare and cook the mole as directed through step 2. Cover and chill for up to 2 days. To serve, place the mole in a small saucepan and heat over medium heat until hot. Continue as directed.

creamy CHICKEN ENCHILADAS

Prep: 30 minutes
Bake: 40 minutes
Stand: 5 minutes
Oven: 350°F
Makes: 6 servings

- 8 ounces skinless, boneless chicken breast halves
- ⅔ cup reduced-sodium chicken broth
- ¼ teaspoon ground black pepper
- 4 cups torn fresh spinach
- 2 tablespoons thinly sliced scallion
- 1¼ cups light sour cream
- 2 tablespoons all-purpose flour
- ½ teaspoon salt
- ½ teaspoon ground cumin
- ½ cup milk
- 1 4-ounce can diced green chile peppers, drained
- 6 7-inch whole wheat flour tortillas
- ½ cup shredded Monterey Jack cheese or cheddar cheese (2 ounces)
  Snipped fresh cilantro (optional)
  Salsa and/or thinly sliced scallion (optional)

1 Preheat oven to 350°F. In a large skillet, combine chicken, broth, and black pepper. Bring to boiling; reduce heat. Simmer, covered, for 12 to 14 minutes or until chicken is no longer pink (170°F); drain. Using two forks, shred chicken into bite-size pieces.

2 Meanwhile, place spinach in a steamer basket. Place basket in a saucepan over 1 inch of boiling water. Steam, covered, for 3 to 5 minutes or until tender. Transfer spinach to a sieve; press out excess liquid with the back of a spoon.

3 For filling, in a large bowl, combine shredded chicken, cooked spinach, and the 2 tablespoons scallion. For sauce, in a small bowl combine sour cream, flour, salt, and cumin. Stir in milk and chile peppers. Stir half of the sauce into filling; set the remaining sauce aside.

4 Grease a 2-quart baking dish. Divide filling among tortillas; roll up tortillas. Arrange tortillas, seam sides down, in the prepared baking dish. Top with the remaining sauce.

5 Bake, covered, for 20 minutes. Bake, uncovered, for about 20 minutes more or until heated through. Sprinkle with cheese. Let stand for 5 minutes before serving. If desired, garnish with cilantro and serve with salsa and/or additional scallion.

Nutrition facts per serving: 251 cal., 9 g total fat (4 g sat. fat), 46 mg chol., 571 mg sodium, 23 g carb., 18 g protein.

chipotle-chicken CASSEROLE

Chipotle chiles are actually smoked jalapeño peppers. Here they add a smoky-hot appeal to this family-style dish. Look for canned chipotles in adobo sauce in the international food aisle of your supermarket or at Hispanic food markets.

Prep: 20 minutes
Bake: 20 minutes
Oven: 375°F
Makes: 4 servings

2 **cups frozen or fresh whole kernel corn**

3 **cups frozen diced hash brown potatoes**

1 **14.5-ounce can diced tomatoes with garlic, basil, and oregano, undrained**

2 **chipotle chile peppers in adobo sauce, chopped (see tip, page 8)**

½ **teaspoon chili powder**

½ **teaspoon ground cumin**

½ **teaspoon dried oregano, crushed**

1 **tablespoon olive oil**

4 **skinless, boneless chicken breast halves (1 pound)**

¼ **teaspoon salt**

¼ **teaspoon chili powder**

¼ **teaspoon ground cumin**

¾ **cup shredded Co-Jack cheese (3 ounces)**

1 Preheat oven to 375°F. Coat a 2-quart round casserole with cooking spray. Coat an unheated large nonstick skillet with cooking spray. Heat skillet over medium-high heat. Add corn; cook for about 5 minutes or until corn begins to lightly brown. Add potatoes; cook and stir for 5 to 8 minutes more or until potatoes begin to brown. Stir in tomatoes, chipotle peppers, the ½ teaspoon chili powder, the ½ teaspoon cumin, and the oregano. Remove from heat; transfer mixture to the prepared casserole.

2 Wipe skillet clean. Add oil to skillet and heat over medium-high heat. Sprinkle chicken evenly with salt, the ¼ teaspoon chili powder, and the ¼ teaspoon cumin. Brown chicken in hot oil for about 6 minutes, turning once to brown both sides. Place chicken on top of potato mixture in casserole.

3 Bake, uncovered, in the preheated oven for about 20 minutes or until bubbly and chicken is no longer pink. Sprinkle with cheese.

Nutrition facts per serving: 460 cal., 15 g total fat (6 g sat. fat), 79 mg chol., 939 mg sodium, 50 g carb., 33 g protein.

grilled lime chicken
WITH PINEAPPLE SALSA

Prep: 20 minutes
Grill: 12 minutes
Makes: 6 servings

- ½ **teaspoon finely shredded lime zest**
- ¼ **cup lime juice**
- 1 **tablespoon vegetable oil**
- ¼ **teaspoon salt**
- ¼ **teaspoon coarsely ground black pepper**
- 6 **skinless, boneless chicken breast halves (about 1¾ pounds)**
- 3 **cups fresh pineapple chunks (1 pound)**
- 1 **cup chopped, seeded tomato (1 large)**
- ½ **cup chopped red onion (1 medium)**
- ½ **cup chopped green or red sweet pepper**
- 1 **4-ounce can diced green chile peppers, drained**
- 2 **tablespoons snipped fresh cilantro**
- ½ **teaspoon finely shredded lime zest**
- 2 **tablespoons lime juice**
- 1 **clove garlic, minced**

1 In a small bowl, stir together ½ teaspoon lime zest, the ¼ cup lime juice, the oil, salt, and black pepper. Brush chicken with lime mixture.

2 Place chicken on the rack of an uncovered grill directly over medium coals. Grill for 12 to 15 minutes or until chicken is no longer pink (170°F), turning and brushing once with lime mixture halfway through grilling. Discard any remaining lime mixture.

3 Meanwhile, for salsa, place pineapple chunks in a food processor or blender. Cover and process or blend until chopped, but not pureed. Transfer pineapple to a large bowl. Stir in tomato, red onion, sweet pepper, green chiles, cilantro, ½ teaspoon lime zest, the 2 tablespoons lime juice, and the garlic. Cover and chill in the refrigerator until serving time. Serve with chicken.

Nutrition facts per serving: 209 cal., 5 g total fat (1 g sat. fat), 66 mg chol., 216 mg sodium, 15 g carb., 28 g protein.

pollo RELLENO

Prep: 20 minutes
Bake: 25 minutes
Oven: 375°F
Makes: 6 servings

6 skinless, boneless chicken breast halves (about 2 pounds total)

⅓ cup cornmeal

½ of a 1.25-ounce package (2 tablespoons) taco seasoning mix

1 egg

1 4-ounce can whole green chile peppers, rinsed, seeded, and cut in half lengthwise (6 pieces total)

2 ounces Monterey Jack cheese, cut into six 2×½-inch sticks

2 tablespoons snipped fresh cilantro or fresh parsley

¼ teaspoon ground black pepper

¼ teaspoon crushed red pepper

½ cup shredded Monterey Jack or cheddar cheese (2 ounces; optional)

1 8-ounce jar taco sauce or salsa

Fresh cilantro sprigs (optional)

1 Preheat oven to 375°F. Place each chicken breast half between two pieces of plastic wrap. Using the flat side of a meat mallet, pound the chicken lightly to about ⅛ inch thick. Remove plastic wrap.

2 In a shallow dish, combine cornmeal and taco seasoning mix. Place egg in another dish; beat lightly.

3 For each roll, place a chile pepper half on a chicken piece. Place a cheese stick on top chile pepper near an edge. Sprinkle with some of the cilantro, black pepper, and red pepper. Fold in the side edges; roll up from edge with the cheese stick.

4 Dip rolls into egg and coat with cornmeal mixture. Place rolls, seam side down, in a shallow baking pan. Bake, uncovered, for 25 to 30 minutes. If desired, sprinkle chicken with shredded cheese. Serve with taco sauce. If desired, garnish with cilantro sprigs.

Nutrition facts per serving: 235 cal., 10 g total fat (3 g sat. fat), 103 mg chol., 769 mg sodium, 13 g carb., 28 g protein.

spicy grilled chicken WITH BAJA BLACK BEANS AND RICE

Prep: 20 minutes
Cook: 15 minutes
Grill: 12 minutes
Stand: 5 minutes
Makes: 6 servings

- 1 teaspoon chili powder
- ½ teaspoon ground cumin
- ½ teaspoon garlic powder
- ¼ teaspoon onion powder
- ¼ teaspoon smoked paprika or regular paprika
- 4 skinless, boneless chicken breast halves (1¼ to 1½ pounds total)
- 2½ cups chicken broth
- 2 cups frozen whole kernel corn
- 1 14.5-ounce can fire-roasted diced tomatoes, undrained
- 1¼ cups long grain rice
- 1 cup canned black beans, rinsed and drained
- 1 4-ounce can diced green chile peppers
- 1 cup chopped zucchini (1 small)
- 1 tablespoon snipped fresh cilantro
  Crumbled Cotija cheese (optional)
  Avocado slices (optional)

1 In a small bowl, combine chili powder, cumin, garlic powder, onion powder, and paprika. Sprinkle evenly over all sides of the chicken breast halves; rub in with your fingers. Set aside.

2 In a 4-quart Dutch oven, combine broth, corn, tomatoes, uncooked rice, beans, and chile peppers. Bring to boiling; reduce heat. Simmer, covered, for 12 minutes. Stir in zucchini. Cook, covered, for 3 to 5 minutes more or until zucchini is crisp-tender. Stir in cilantro.

3 Meanwhile, for a charcoal grill, grill chicken breasts on the lightly greased rack of an uncovered grill directly over medium coals for 12 to 15 minutes or until tender and no longer pink (170°F), turning once halfway through grilling. (For a gas grill, preheat grill. Reduce heat to medium. Place chicken on the lightly greased grill rack over heat. Cover and grill as above.)

4 Transfer chicken to a cutting board. Let stand for 5 minutes; slice each breast half. Serve chicken with rice mixture. If desired, pass cheese and avocado.

Nutrition facts per serving: 355 cal., 2 g total fat (0 g sat. fat), 56 mg chol., 796 mg sodium, 54 g carb., 31 g protein.

chicken GUADALAJARA

Prep: 15 minutes
Cook: 13 minutes
Makes: 4 servings

¼ **cup all-purpose flour**

¼ **teaspoon salt**

¼ **teaspoon pepper**

12 **ounces skinless, boneless chicken breast halves, cut into bite-size strips**

3 **tablespoons butter or margarine**

2 **fresh Anaheim chile peppers, seeded and sliced into rings (about 1½ cups)**

1 **medium onion, sliced and separated into rings (½ cup)**

¼ **to ½ teaspoon crushed red pepper**

¾ **cup half-and-half or light cream**

⅓ **cup shredded Monterey Jack cheese**

2 **cups hot cooked fettuccine**

① In a plastic bag combine the flour, salt, and pepper. Add chicken strips to the bag and shake bag to coat chicken.

② In a large skillet heat 2 tablespoons of the butter over medium heat until hot. Add coated chicken strips and cook about 8 minutes or until chicken is tender and no longer pink and coating is golden brown, stirring occasionally. Remove chicken from skillet; keep warm.

③ Heat remaining butter in skillet until hot. Add chili peppers, onion, and crushed red pepper. Cook and stir about 5 minutes or until tender but not brown, stirring up any browned bits. Add cream to skillet. Bring just to boiling. Return chicken to skillet; stir until combined. Simmer, uncovered, for 1 minute more or until slightly thickened.

④ Transfer chicken mixture to a serving dish. Sprinkle with cheese. Cover and let stand 2 to 3 minutes or until cheese is melted. Serve over hot cooked fettuccine.

Nutrition facts per serving: 392 cal., 19 g total fat (11 g sat. fat), 100 mg chol., 294 mg sodium, 28 g carb., 1 g sugar, 27 g protein.

chicken pizza WITH A KICK

Prep: 25 minutes
Bake: 13 minutes
Oven: 400°F
Makes: 6 servings

12 ounces skinless, boneless
   chicken breast halves,
   cut into thin strips

2 teaspoons cooking oil

1 medium red sweet pepper,
   cut into thin strips

½ of a medium red onion,
   thinly sliced

1 10-ounce package
   refrigerated pizza dough

½ cup bottled mild picante
   sauce or taco sauce

½ cup shredded sharp
   cheddar cheese
   (2 ounces)

1 Preheat oven to 400°F. In a large nonstick skillet, cook chicken strips in hot oil over medium-high heat for about 5 minutes or until no longer pink. Remove from skillet. Add sweet pepper and onion to skillet; cook for about 5 minutes or until tender. Remove from skillet; set aside.

2 Coat a 15×10×1-inch baking pan with nonstick cooking spray. Unroll pizza dough into pan; press with fingers to form a 12×8-inch rectangle. Pinch edges of dough to form crust.

3 Spread crust with picante sauce. Top with chicken and vegetables; sprinkle with cheddar cheese. Bake for 13 to 18 minutes or until crust is brown and cheese melts.

Nutrition facts per serving: 305 cal., 9 g total fat (3 g sat. fat), 43 mg chol., 527 mg sodium, 34 g carb., 21 g protein.

chicken AND BEAN TACOS

When you need dinner in a hurry, these hearty tacos go together in next to no time.

Start to Finish: 25 minutes
Oven: 375°F
Makes: 4 servings

8 taco shells or 6-inch
   flour tortillas

1 3.25-ounce can bean dip

6 ounces sliced cooked
   chicken breast or
   turkey breast

2 cups shredded lettuce
   or purchased torn
   mixed greens

1 2.25-ounce can sliced
   pitted black olives,
   drained

1 cup shredded cheddar or
   Monterey Jack cheese
   (4 ounces)

   Chunky salsa (optional)

   Sour cream (optional)

1 Preheat oven to 375°F. Wrap taco shells or tortillas in foil; place on a baking sheet. Bake for 5 minutes. Heat bean dip according to directions on can. Meanwhile, stack chicken slices; roll up in a spiral. Cut roll crosswise into eight pieces; use your fingers to shred slightly.

2 To assemble tacos, spread 1 to 2 tablespoons heated bean dip onto bottom of one of the taco shells (if using); top with lettuce. Add chicken pieces, olives, and cheese. (If using tortillas, place each tortilla on a flat surface; sprinkle ingredients down center. Fold sides over filling.) If desired, serve tacos topped with salsa and sour cream.

Nutrition facts per serving: 359 cal., 19 g total fat (8 g sat. fat), 66 mg chol., 546 mg sodium, 23 g carb., 24 g protein.

tex-mex chicken 'N' RICE CASSEROLE

A package of rice and vermicelli mix gets the flavors hopping in this crowd-pleaser. The supportive cast of ingredients, including chile peppers, chili powder, and cumin, contribute to the potent Tex-Mex flavor.

Prep: 20 minutes
Bake: 25 minutes
Stand: 5 minutes
Oven: 425°F
Makes: 6 servings

½ cup chopped onion
   (1 medium)

1 tablespoon olive oil

1 6.9-ounce package
   chicken-flavor rice and
   vermicelli mix

1 14-ounce can
   chicken broth

2 cups water

2 cups chopped cooked
   chicken (10 ounces)

1 cup chopped seeded
   tomatoes (2 medium)

3 tablespoons canned
   diced green chile
   peppers, drained

1½ teaspoons chili powder

1 teaspoon dried
   basil, crushed

⅛ teaspoon ground cumin

⅛ teaspoon ground
   black pepper

½ cup shredded cheddar
   cheese (2 ounces)

1 Preheat oven to 425°F. In a medium saucepan, cook onion in hot oil over medium heat until tender. Stir in rice and vermicelli mix (including contents of the seasoning packet). Cook and stir for 2 minutes. Stir in broth and the water. Bring to boiling; reduce heat. Simmer, covered, for 20 minutes (liquid will not be fully absorbed).

2 Transfer the rice mixture to a large bowl. Stir in chicken, tomatoes, chile peppers, chili powder, basil, cumin, and black pepper. Transfer to an ungreased 2-quart casserole.

3 Bake, covered, for about 25 minutes or until heated through. Uncover and sprinkle with cheese. Let stand for 5 minutes before serving.

Nutrition facts per serving: 323 cal., 14 g total fat (4 g sat. fat), 53 mg chol., 971 mg sodium, 30 g carb., 21 g protein.

layered chicken AND
CHILE CASSEROLE

Patterned after a popular Texas recipe, this irresistible main dish includes seasoned chicken layered with chile peppers, tortillas, sour cream sauce, and cheese.

Prep: 20 minutes
Bake: 35 minutes
Stand: 10 minutes
Oven: 350°F
Makes: 12 servings

2 **tomatillos**

1 **cup chopped onion**

4 **teaspoon chili powder**

2 **cloves garlic, minced**

2 **tablespoons cooking oil**

2 **10.75-ounce cans condensed cream of chicken soup**

2 **4-ounce cans diced green chile peppers, drained**

2 **4-ounce jars diced pimientos, drained**

½ **cup sour cream**

12 **6-inch corn tortillas, torn**

3 **cups cubed cooked chicken**

2 **cups shredded Monterey Jack cheese (8 ounces)**

Salsa verde (optional)

1 Preheat oven to 350°F. Remove and discard the thin, brown, papery husks from the tomatillos. Rinse tomatillos; finely chop (you should have about ½ cup). For sauce, in a medium saucepan cook chopped tomatillos, onion, chili powder, and garlic in hot oil over medium heat until vegetables are tender. Remove from heat; stir in soup, chile peppers, pimiento, and sour cream.

2 Spread ½ cup of the sauce in the bottom of a 3-quart rectangular baking dish. Arrange half of the torn corn tortillas over the sauce. Layer with half of the chicken, half of the remaining sauce, and half of the cheese. Repeat layers.

3 Bake, covered, for 35 to 40 minutes or until heated through. Let stand for 10 minutes before serving (if toting, see note). If desired, serve with salsa verde.

Nutrition facts per serving: 297 cal., 16 g total fat (7 g sat. fat), 55 mg chol., 663 mg sodium, 20 g carb., 19 g protein.

To Tote: Do not let stand after baking. Cover tightly. Transport in an insulated carrier. If desired, transport salsa in an insulated cooler with ice packs.

enchiladas SUIZAS

Prep: 40 minutes
Bake: 25 minutes
Stand: 10 minutes
Oven: Broil/350°F
Makes: 12 enchiladas

- 1 purchased
  roasted chicken
- 12 ounces fresh tomatillos
  (4 large), husks removed
- ½ of a medium onion, cut
  into thin wedges
- 2 fresh jalapeño chile
  peppers (see tip, page 8)
- 2 cloves garlic
- 1 14.5-ounce can diced
  fire-roasted tomatoes,
  undrained
- ¾ cup packed fresh
  cilantro sprigs
- 1 cup Mexican crema or one
  8-ounce carton crème
  fraîche or sour cream
- 1 tablespoon all-purpose
  flour
- ¼ teaspoon salt
- 12 6-inch corn tortillas
- 2 tablespoons vegetable oil
- 3 ounces Chihuahua cheese
  or Monterey Jack cheese,
  shredded (¾ cup)
  Fresh cilantro sprigs
  (optional)

1 Preheat broiler. Carve or pull meat from the chicken; using two forks, pull meat apart into shreds. Measure 2½ cups of the chicken for this recipe. (Save any remaining chicken for another use.)

2 On a large baking sheet, combine tomatillos, onion wedges, chile peppers, and garlic. Broil 3 inches from heat about 14 minutes or until tender with black spots and blistered skin on peppers, turning once during broiling. Cool slightly. With gloved hands, use a paring knife to peel as much skin from the peppers as possible; halve and seed peppers. Core tomatillos. Reduce oven temperature to 350°F; adjust oven rack to center of oven.

3 In a blender, combine vegetables, fire-roasted tomatoes, and cilantro. Cover and blend until smooth. Add crema, flour, and salt. Cover and blend briefly until smooth.

4 In a medium bowl, combine shredded chicken and ½ cup of the tomatillo-crema mixture. Spread about ½ cup of the remaining tomatillo-crema mixture in the bottom of a 3-quart rectangular baking dish; set aside.

5 Wash and dry the baking sheet; lay tortillas on baking sheet. Brush both sides of each tortilla lightly with oil. Bake for 2 to 3 minutes or just until softened. Remove from oven. Stack tortillas and wrap in foil.

6 Removing one tortilla at a time, divide chicken-tomatillo mixture among tortillas, spreading evenly over each tortilla. Roll up tortillas. Arrange rolled tortillas, seam sides down, in the prepared baking dish. Pour the remaining tomatillo-crema mixture over tortillas. Top with shredded cheese. Bake, uncovered, about 25 minutes or until heated through and cheese starts to brown lightly. Let stand for 10 minutes before serving. Garnish with cilantro sprigs, if desired.

Nutrition facts per enchilada: 357 cal., 23 g total fat (9 g sat. fat), 108 mg chol., 736 mg sodium, 18 g carb., 22 g protein.

mexican CHICKEN CASSEROLE

All it takes are four simple ingredients to dress up a store-bought roasted chicken for a Mexican fiesta. Serve some guacamole and Spanish rice on the side.

Prep: 15 minutes
Bake: 15 minutes
Oven: 350°F
Makes: 4 servings

1 **15-ounce can black beans, rinsed and drained**
½ **cup chunky salsa**
½ **teaspoon ground cumin**
1 **2- to 2½-pound whole deli-roasted chicken**
¼ **cup shredded Monterey Jack cheese with jalapeño chile peppers (1 ounce)**
   Sour cream (optional)

① Preheat oven to 350°F. In a small bowl, stir together beans, ¼ cup of the salsa, and the cumin. Divide bean mixture among four individual au gratin dishes or casseroles.

② Cut chicken into quarters. Place one chicken quarter on bean mixture in each dish. Spoon the remaining salsa evenly over chicken pieces. Sprinkle with cheese.

③ Bake for 15 to 20 minutes or until heated through. If desired, serve with sour cream.

Nutrition facts per serving: 468 cal., 23 g total fat (7 g sat. fat), 140 mg chol., 596 mg sodium, 16 g carb., 50 g protein.

nacho turkey CASSEROLE

Prep: 20 minutes
Bake: 30 minutes
Oven: 350°F
Makes: 8 servings

5   cups slightly crushed tortilla chips

4   cups cubed cooked turkey or chicken (about 1¼ pounds)

2   16-ounce jars salsa

1   10-ounce package frozen whole kernel corn

½   cup sour cream

2   tablespoons all-purpose flour

1   cup shredded Monterey Jack cheese with jalapeño chile peppers or mozzarella cheese (4 ounces)

1 Preheat oven to 350°F. Place 3 cups of the tortilla chips in a greased 3-quart rectangular baking dish. In a large bowl, combine turkey, salsa, corn, sour cream, and flour; spoon over tortilla chips.

2 Bake, uncovered, for 25 minutes. Sprinkle with the remaining 2 cups tortilla chips and the cheese. Bake for 5 to 10 minutes more or until heated through.

Nutrition facts per serving: 444 cal., 17 g total fat (7 g sat. fat), 74 mg chol., 1127 mg sodium, 46 g carb., 29 g protein.

turkey WITH MOLE

Prep: 1½ hours
Bake: 1½ hours
Oven: 350°F
Makes: 8 to 10 servings

3 dried ancho chile peppers (see tip, page 8)

2 dried pasilla chile peppers (see tip, page 8)

2 dried mulato chile peppers (see tip, page 8)

3 cups hot chicken broth

⅓ cup blanched whole almonds

1 6-inch corn tortilla

2 tablespoons sesame seeds

¼ teaspoon coriander seeds

¼ teaspoon anise seeds

½ of a 14.5-ounce can diced tomatoes, undrained

½ cup chopped onion (1 medium)

¼ cup raisins

1 ounce unsweetened chocolate, chopped

1 clove garlic

½ teaspoon ground cinnamon

⅛ teaspoon ground black pepper

Pinch ground cloves

1 tablespoon lard

1 tablespoon sugar

1 teaspoon salt

2 tablespoons lard

1 8- to 10-pound turkey, cut up

1. For mole, in a well-ventilated area, in a dry skillet over medium heat, toast dried peppers, turning occasionally until they have a toasted aroma, about 8 minutes. Let cool. Discard stems, seeds, and ribs from peppers. Place peppers in a bowl. Cover with hot broth. Let stand for 30 minutes to soften. Strain soaking liquid through 100% cotton cheesecloth; reserve soaking liquid (you should have about 2½ cups). Cut peppers into pieces.

2. Preheat oven to 350°F. In a dry skillet individually toast almonds, tortilla, sesame seeds, coriander seeds, and anise seeds over medium heat for 1 to 3 minutes, stirring or turning frequently. Watch seeds carefully so they do not burn. Tear up toasted tortilla.

3. In a large bowl, combine drained peppers, almonds, torn tortilla, seeds, tomatoes, onion, raisins, chocolate, garlic, cinnamon, black pepper, and cloves. In a blender or food processor, blend or process the pepper mixture, half at a time, to make a coarse puree.

4. In a medium saucepan, heat 1 tablespoon lard over medium heat. Add mole puree; cook about 5 minutes or until darkened and thick, stirring often. Slowly stir in 1¼ cups of the reserved soaking liquid. Cook and stir over medium-low heat for 5 minutes or until mixture is the consistency of heavy cream. Stir in sugar and salt.

5. In a 12-inch skillet, heat 2 tablespoons lard over medium-high heat. Brown turkey pieces, about half at a time, for 3 to 4 minutes per side. Place in a roasting pan. Coat all surfaces of the turkey pieces with 2 cups of the mole.

6. Bake, covered, for 1½ to 2 hours or until turkey is tender, no longer pink inside, and a thermometer registers 170°F in breasts and 180°F in drumsticks and thighs. Reheat remaining mole and serve with turkey.

Nutrition facts per serving: 482 cal., 26 g total fat (8 g sat. fat), 121 mg chol., 729 mg sodium, 18 g carb., 45 g protein.

turkey ENCHILADAS

Prep: 20 minutes
Bake: 1 hour
Oven: 375°F
Makes: 8 servings

2 to 2½ cups shredded
   cooked turkey

1 14.5-ounce can no-salt-
   added diced tomatoes

1 15-ounce can black beans,
   rinsed

1½ cups bottled salsa

¾ cup shredded Co-Jack
   cheese (3 ounces)

½ cup light sour cream

3 scallions, sliced

¼ cup chopped
   fresh cilantro

1 teaspoon ground cumin

½ teaspoon salt

½ teaspoon ground
   black pepper

8 7- to 8-inch whole wheat
   or regular flour tortillas

1 teaspoon bottled hot
   pepper sauce

Fresh cilantro leaves

Scallions, chopped

1 Preheat oven to 375°F. Lightly coat a 3-quart rectangular baking dish with cooking spray. For filling, stir together turkey, half the tomatoes with juice, beans, ½ cup salsa, ½ cup cheese, sour cream, scallions, cilantro, cumin, salt, and pepper. Spoon about ⅔ cup filling on each tortilla. Roll tortillas around filling. Place, seam sides down, in prepared dish.

2 For sauce, stir together remaining tomatoes and juice, salsa, and hot pepper sauce. Spoon over enchiladas. Cover dish with foil and bake for 30 minutes. Uncover and top with remaining cheese; bake for 5 to 10 minutes more or until heated through and cheese is melted. Sprinkle with additional cilantro and scallions.

Nutrition facts per serving: 305 cal., 26 g total fat (4.5 g sat. fat), 40 mg chol., 871 mg sodium, 29 g carb., 26 g protein.

layered turkey ENCHILADAS

Start to Finish: 20 minutes
Oven: 450°F
Makes: 4 servings

1 pound turkey breast tenderloin, cut in bite-size strips

1 tablespoon cooking oil

1 16-ounce package frozen sweet peppers and onions stir-fry vegetables

1 10-ounce can enchilada sauce

½ cup whole berry cranberry sauce

Salt and ground black pepper

9 6-inch corn tortillas, halved

1 8-ounce package Mexican-blend shredded cheese (2 cups)

Lime wedges (optional)

Fresh cilantro sprigs (optional)

1 Position oven rack toward top of oven. Preheat oven to 450°F. In extra-large skillet, cook turkey in hot oil over medium heat for 4 minutes or until no longer pink. Add frozen vegetables, enchilada sauce, and cranberry sauce. Bring to boiling. Sprinkle with salt and pepper.

2 In 2-quart baking dish, layer one-third of the tortillas, then one-third of the cheese. Use a slotted spoon to layer half the turkey-vegetable mixture. Layer one-third tortillas, one-third cheese, remaining turkey-vegetables (with slotted spoon), and remaining tortillas. Spoon on remaining sauce from skillet; sprinkle with remaining cheese. Bake for 5 minutes or until cheese is melted. Cut into squares. Serve with lime wedges and cilantro.

Nutrition facts per serving: 615 cal., 25 g total fat (11 g sat. fat), 120 mg chol., 1171 mg sodium, 52 g carb., 45 g protein.

grilled turkey WITH CORN, TOMATO, AND SWEET PEPPER SALSA

Prep: 15 minutes
Chill: 1 hour
Grill: 4 minutes
Makes: 4 servings

1½ **pounds ripe tomatoes, seeded and chopped**

1½ **cups fresh corn kernels**

1 **large red sweet pepper, seeded and chopped**

¾ **cup fresh cilantro leaves, coarsely chopped**

1 **fresh jalapeño chile pepper, seeded and finely chopped (see tip, page 8)**

2 **tablespoons extra-virgin olive oil**

2 **tablespoons lime juice**

¾ **teaspoon salt**

1¼ **pounds turkey cutlets**

¼ **teaspoon ground black pepper**

Lime wedges

1 In a large bowl, stir together tomatoes, corn, sweet pepper, cilantro, jalapeño, olive oil, lime juice, and ½ teaspoon of the salt. Cover and refrigerate for 1 hour.

2 Heat grill to medium-high. Season the turkey with the remaining ¼ teaspoon salt and the black pepper.

3 Grill turkey for about 2 minutes per side or until cooked through. Serve warm or at room temperature with the salsa and lime wedges.

Nutrition facts per serving: 462 cal., 12 g total fat (4 g sat. fat), 67 mg chol., 461 mg sodium, 53 g carb., 34 g protein.

fish
& SEAFOOD

Shrimp Tacos, *page 178*

broiled TUNA FAJITAS

Prep: 20 minutes
Marinate: 30 minutes
Broil: 8 minutes
Makes: 4 servings

- 2 5- to 6-ounce fresh or frozen tuna or halibut steaks, cut 1 inch thick
- ¼ cup lime juice
- 2 tablespoons snipped fresh cilantro or parsley
- 1 tablespoon olive oil
- 2 cloves garlic, minced
- ¼ teaspoon coarsely ground black pepper
- ⅛ teaspoon cayenne pepper
- 8 6-inch corn tortillas
- 2 medium red and/or yellow sweet peppers, quartered and stems and seeds removed
- 1 cup tomato salsa or tomatillo salsa

1 Thaw fish, if frozen. Rinse fish; pat dry with paper towels. Place fish in a heavy, large resealable plastic bag set in a shallow dish.

2 For marinade, in a small bowl stir together lime juice, cilantro, oil, garlic, black pepper, and cayenne. Pour marinade over fish in bag. Seal bag; turn to coat fish. Marinate in the refrigerator for 30 minutes, turning bag occasionally.

3 Wrap tortillas tightly in foil. Drain fish, reserving marinade. Lightly coat the unheated rack of a broiler pan with nonstick cooking spray. Place fish on prepared broiler pan. Place sweet pepper quarters beside fish. Place wrapped tortillas alongside the broiler pan. Broil 4 to 5 inches from heat for 8 to 12 minutes or just until fish flakes easily when tested with a fork, brushing once with reserved marinade after 3 minutes of broiling and turning once halfway through broiling. Discard any remaining marinade. Broil sweet peppers for about 8 minutes or until tender, turning occasionally. Broil tortillas for about 8 minutes or until heated through, turning once.

4 Using a fork, break fish into large chunks. Cut sweet peppers into ½-inch-wide strips. Immediately fill warm tortillas with fish and sweet pepper strips. Serve with salsa.

Nutrition facts per serving: 285 cal., 9 g total fat (2 g sat. fat), 27 mg chol., 440 mg sodium, 33 g carb., 21 g protein.

grilled halibut
SARANDEADO

Prep: 20 minutes
Marinate: 30 minutes
Grill: 4 minutes per ½-inch thickness
Makes: 4 servings

4 6-ounce fresh or frozen halibut or grouper fillets

½ cup Mexican lemon juice or regular lemon juice

1 medium fresh serrano chile pepper, seeded and chopped (see tip, page 8)

1 tablespoon Worcestershire sauce

½ teaspoon coarse salt

½ teaspoon ground black pepper

¼ cup coarsely snipped fresh cilantro

Salt and ground black pepper

1 grilled lemon (Mexican lemon, if possible), cut into wedges

Grilled scallions (optional)

1 Thaw fish, if frozen. Rinse fish; pat dry with paper towels. Place fish fillets in a resealable plastic bag set in a shallow dish.

2 In a blender, combine lemon juice, serrano pepper, Worcestershire sauce, coarse salt, and the ½ teaspoon black pepper. Cover and blend until smooth. Pour lemon juice mixture over fish. Seal bag; turn to coat fish. Marinate in the refrigerator for 30 minutes, turning once. (Do not marinate longer than 30 minutes.) Drain, reserving marinade.

3 For a charcoal grill, grill fish on the lightly greased rack of an uncovered grill directly over medium coals for 4 to 6 minutes per ½-inch thickness or until fish flakes easily when tested with a fork, turning and brushing with reserved marinade once halfway through grilling. Discard any remaining marinade. (For a gas grill, preheat grill. Reduce heat to medium. Place fish on greased grill rack over heat. Cover and grill as above.)

4 Sprinkle fish with cilantro. Season to taste with salt and black pepper. Serve with lemon wedges and, if desired, grilled scallions.

Nutrition facts per serving: 176 cal., 2 g total fat (0 g sat. fat), 63 mg chol., 481 mg sodium, 7 g carb., 34 g protein.

fish TACOS

Many dishes that originate in the Yucatán peninsula—between the Caribbean Sea and the Gulf of Mexico—take advantage of the seas' bounty. Don't marinate the fish for more than 30 minutes; if it sits much longer, the acidic lime juice will "cook" it.

Prep: 25 minutes
Marinate: 30 minutes
Bake: 10 minutes
Broil: 8 minutes
Oven: 350°F
Makes: 4 servings

- 1 **pound fresh or frozen firm-flesh fish fillets, such as halibut, 1 inch thick**
- ¼ **cup tequila, lime juice, or lemon juice**
- 2 **tablespoons lime juice or lemon juice**
- 1 **fresh jalapeño or serrano chile pepper, seeded and finely chopped (see tip, page 8)**
- ¼ **teaspoon ground cumin**
- 2 **cloves garlic, minced**
- 24 **4-inch corn tortillas, or eight 8-inch flour tortillas**
- 1½ **cups shredded lettuce**
- 1 **cup chopped red or green sweet pepper**
- 1 **medium red onion, halved and thinly sliced**

  Snipped fresh cilantro (optional)

  Mango or papaya slices (optional)

1 Thaw fish, if frozen. Rinse fish; pat dry. Place fish in a shallow dish. For marinade, in a small bowl stir together tequila, lime juice, jalapeño pepper, cumin, and garlic. Pour marinade over fish. Cover and marinate in the refrigerator for 30 minutes, turning fish occasionally.

2 Preheat oven to 350°F. Wrap tortillas tightly in foil. Heat in oven about 10 minutes or until heated through.

3 Preheat broiler. Drain fish; discard marinade. Pat fish dry. Place fish on the greased unheated rack of a broiler pan. Broil 4 inches from the heat for 5 minutes. Using a wide spatula, carefully turn the fish. Broil for 3 to 7 minutes more or just until fish flakes easily when tested with a fork. (Or place fish fillets in a well-greased wire grill basket. Grill on the rack of an uncovered grill directly over medium coals for 8 to 12 minutes or just until fish flakes easily when tested with a fork, turning once.)

4 With a fork, break broiled fish into ½-inch chunks. To assemble tacos, place lettuce in center of each warm tortilla. Divide fish chunks, sweet pepper, and red onion among tortillas. Fold tortillas in half over filling. If desired, serve with cilantro and mango slices.

Nutrition facts per serving: 276 cal., 5 g total fat (1 g sat. fat), 22 mg chol., 314 mg sodium, 34 g carb., 21 g protein.

red SNAPPER ADOBO

Prep: 35 minutes
Stand: 15 minutes
Marinate: 1 to 24 hours
Grill: 12 minutes
Makes: 4 servings

4 6- to 8-ounce fresh or frozen boneless red snapper fillets

¼ cup canola oil or vegetable oil

5 dried ancho chile peppers (about 3 ounces), stemmed, seeded, and quartered (see tip, page 8)

1¾ cups hot water

15 sprigs fresh cilantro

¼ cup lime juice

¼ cup cider vinegar

5 cloves garlic

2 tablespoons paprika

2 tablespoons packed dark brown sugar

2 tablespoons sesame seeds

1 tablespoon kosher salt

1 teaspoon ground black pepper

½ teaspoon ground cinnamon

¼ teaspoon ground cloves

Lime wedges

1 Thaw fish, if frozen. Rinse fish; pat dry with paper towels. Set aside.

2 For marinade, in a large saucepan heat oil over medium heat. Add one-third of the chile peppers. Cook about 10 seconds or just until skins begin to blister. Remove chiles with slotted spoon. Repeat with the remaining chile peppers. Reserve oil in saucepan; transfer chile peppers to a blender or food processor. Add the hot water to blender or processor. Let stand for 15 to 20 minutes or until peppers are softened.

3 Add cilantro sprigs, lime juice, vinegar, garlic, paprika, brown sugar, sesame seeds, salt, black pepper, cinnamon, and cloves to pepper mixture in blender or processor. Cover and blend or process until smooth. Press mixture through a medium-mesh sieve set over a bowl; discard solids. Stir the reserved oil into pepper liquid; set aside.

4 Score the fish skin by making three diagonal slashes across each fillet; transfer fish to a shallow dish. Wearing gloves, use hands to smear both sides of each fillet with the marinade, being sure to get marinade into the slashes. Cover and chill for 1 to 24 hours.

5 Tear off four 28×18-inch pieces of heavy-duty foil; fold each piece in half to make four 18×14-inch rectangles. Divide fish and marinade among the four rectangles. For each packet, bring up two opposite edges of foil and seal with a double fold. Fold remaining edges together to completely enclose fish, leaving space for steam to build. For a charcoal grill, grill the foil packets on rack of an uncovered grill directly over medium-hot coals for 12 minutes or until the fish flakes easily with a fork, turning packets once halfway through cooking and opening one pouch to check for doneness.

6 Serve fish with lime wedges.

Nutrition facts per serving: 433 cal., 20 g total fat (2 g sat. fat), 63 mg chol., 1573 mg sodium, 26 g carb., 39 g protein.

snapper VERACRUZ

Start to Finish: 30 minutes
Makes: 6 servings

1½ pounds fresh or frozen skinless red snapper or other fish fillets, ½ to ¾ inch thick

⅛ teaspoon salt

⅛ teaspoon ground black pepper

1 large onion, sliced and separated into rings

2 cloves garlic, minced

1 tablespoon cooking oil

2 large tomatoes, chopped

¼ cup sliced pimiento-stuffed green olives

¼ cup dry white wine

2 tablespoons capers, drained

1 to 2 fresh jalapeño or serrano chile peppers, seeded and chopped, or 1 to 2 canned jalapeño chile peppers, rinsed, drained, seeded, and chopped (see tip, page 8)

½ teaspoon sugar

1 bay leaf

Snipped fresh parsley

1 Thaw fish, if frozen. Rinse fish; pat dry with paper towels. Cut into six serving-size pieces, if necessary. Sprinkle fish with salt and black pepper.

2 For sauce, in a large skillet cook onion and garlic in hot oil until onion is tender. Stir in tomatoes, olives, wine, capers, chile peppers, sugar, and bay leaf. Bring to boiling. Add fish to skillet. Return to boiling; reduce heat. Cover and simmer for 6 to 10 minutes or until fish flakes easily when tested with a fork. Use a slotted spatula to carefully transfer fish from skillet to a serving platter. Cover and keep warm.

3 Boil sauce in skillet for 5 to 6 minutes or until reduced to about 2 cups, stirring occasionally. Discard bay leaf. Spoon sauce over fish. Sprinkle with parsley.

Nutrition facts per serving: 174 cal., 5 g total fat (1 g sat. fat), 42 mg chol., 260 mg sodium, 7 g carb., 24 g protein.

mahi mahi WITH BLACK BEAN AND AVOCADO RELISH

A squeeze of fresh lime brightens the flavor of the black bean and avocado relish.

Prep: 20 minutes
Grill: 4 minutes
Makes: 4 servings

- 1 **pound fresh or frozen skinless mahi mahi fillets**
- 2 **tablespoons snipped fresh cilantro**
- 2 **tablespoons snipped fresh oregano**
- ½ **teaspoon finely shredded lime zest**
- 2 **tablespoons lime juice**
- 1 **tablespoon olive oil**
- 1 **to 2 cloves garlic, minced**
- ¼ **to ½ teaspoon bottled hot pepper sauce**
- 1 **15-ounce can black beans, rinsed and drained**
- 1 **medium avocado, pitted, peeled, and chopped**
  Salt and ground black pepper
  Fresh oregano sprig (optional)

1 Thaw fish, if frozen. Rinse fish; pat dry with paper towels. Cut into four serving-size pieces. In a small bowl, combine cilantro, oregano, lime zest, lime juice, oil, garlic, and hot pepper sauce. For relish, in a medium bowl combine beans and avocado; stir in half of the cilantro mixture. Cover and chill until ready to serve.

2 Measure thickness of fish fillets; sprinkle fish lightly with salt and black pepper. Brush the remaining cilantro mixture over all sides of the fish fillets. For a charcoal grill, grill fish on the greased rack of an uncovered grill directly over medium coals for 4 to 6 minutes per ½-inch thickness or until fish flakes easily when tested with a fork, carefully turning halfway through grilling. (For a gas grill, preheat grill. Reduce heat to medium. Place fish on greased grill rack over heat. Cover and grill as above.)

3 To serve, arrange fish on top of relish; garnish with an oregano sprig, if desired.

Nutrition facts per serving: 255 cal., 10 g total fat (1 g sat. fat), 83 mg chol., 369 mg sodium, 18 g carb., 29 g protein.

creamy cheesy SALMON ENCHILADAS

Prep: 25 minutes
Bake: 35 minutes
Oven: 375°F
Makes: 6 servings

1 3-ounce package cream cheese, softened

1 8-ounce package shredded Mexican-style four-cheese blend (2 cups)

1 16-ounce jar salsa

1 4-ounce can diced green chile peppers, drained

2 14.75-ounce cans salmon, drained, flaked, and skin and bones removed

6 10- to 12-inch flour tortillas

1 Preheat oven to 375°F. In a large bowl, stir together cream cheese, 1 cup of the Mexican cheese blend, 2 tablespoons of the salsa, and the chile peppers. Fold in salmon. Spoon about ¾ cup filling across each tortilla slightly below center. Fold in ends and roll up. Place in a 3-quart rectangular baking dish. Top with remaining salsa and cheese.

2 Bake, covered, for 25 minutes. Uncover and bake for about 10 minutes more or until heated through.

Nutrition facts per serving: 547 cal., 29 g total fat (13 g sat. fat), 125 mg chol., 1820 mg sodium, 29 g carb., 41 g protein.

chipotle SALMON TACOS

Leftover chipotle peppers and sauce can be frozen. Freeze them in small containers in portions of one or two peppers so you can just thaw what you need next time you cook with them.

Prep: 10 minutes
Bake: 18 minutes
Oven: 450°F
Makes: 4 (2-taco) servings

1 **1¼-pound fresh or frozen salmon fillet, with skin**

¼ **teaspoon salt**

1 **canned chipotle chile pepper in adobo sauce, seeded, chopped, and mixed with 1 tablespoon adobo sauce (see tip, page 8)**

8 **taco shells**

1 **11-ounce can whole kernel corn with sweet peppers**

1 **cup hot salsa**

1 Thaw fish, if frozen. Preheat oven to 450°F. Rinse fish; pat dry with paper towels. Place fish, skin side down, in a 2-quart rectangular baking dish. Sprinkle with salt. Spread chipotle pepper and sauce over fish.

2 Bake for about 18 minutes or until fish begins to flake when tested with a fork. Add taco shells to the oven for the last 3 minutes of baking.

3 Meanwhile, in a small saucepan, heat corn over medium heat. Remove fish from oven; flake fish.

4 Divide corn and fish among warm taco shells. Serve with salsa.

Nutrition facts per serving: 349 cal., 10 g total fat (2 g sat. fat), 66 mg chol., 1079 mg sodium, 31 g carb., 32 g protein.

ancho-glazed salmon
WITH SWEET POTATO FRIES

Ground ancho chile adds a delicious bite to grilled fish.

Prep: 15 minutes
Start to Finish: 20 minutes
Makes: 4 servings

- 2 **medium sweet potatoes, scrubbed**
- 1 **tablespoon sugar**
- 1 **teaspoon salt**
- 1 **teaspoon ground cumin**
- 1 **teaspoon ground ancho chile or chili powder**
  Nonstick cooking spray
- 4 **5-ounce skinless salmon fillets**
- 1 **tablespoon olive oil**
  Fresh cilantro sprigs

1 Preheat broiler and cut potatoes lengthwise into ¼-inch-thick slices. Combine sugar, salt, cumin, and ancho chile. Place sweet potatoes on the greased rack of an unheated broiler pan. Coat both sides of potato slices with cooking spray; sprinkle both sides with about half the sugar mixture. Broil 4 to 6 inches from heat for 10 minutes or until tender, turning once.

2 Meanwhile, rinse salmon, pat dry, and sprinkle with remaining sugar mixture. In a large skillet, cook salmon in hot oil over medium heat, turning once halfway through cooking, for 8 to 12 minutes or until fish flakes easily when tested with a fork. Serve potatoes and salmon with cilantro sprigs.

Nutrition facts per serving: 363 cal., 19 g total fat (3.5 g sat. fat), 84 mg chol., 710 mg sodium, 17 g carb., 29 g protein.

rollos DEL MAR

Prep: 35 minutes
Stand: 20 minutes
Bake: 25 minutes
Oven: 400°F
Makes: 6 servings

8 ounces fresh or frozen shrimp in shells

6 4- to 6-ounce fresh or frozen skinless grouper or red snapper fillets

4 ounces fresh or frozen squid, scallops, or peeled and deveined shrimp

1 dried ancho chile pepper, stemmed, seeded, and cut into pieces (see tip, page 8)

3 tablespoons butter

1 cup chopped onion (1 large)

8 cloves garlic, minced

1 14.5-ounce can fire-roasted diced tomatoes, drained

¼ cup chicken broth or vegetable broth

2 tablespoons whipping cream

¼ teaspoon salt

⅛ teaspoon ground black pepper

2 tablespoons snipped fresh parsley

6 slices thinly sliced serrano ham or prosciutto

1 Thaw seafood, if frozen. Peel and devein shrimp. Rinse seafood; pat dry with paper towels. Chop shrimp and squid. Set aside.

2 For sauce, place chile pepper pieces in a small bowl. Add enough boiling water to cover. Let stand for 20 minutes to soften pepper. Drain and set aside. In a large skillet melt 2 tablespoons of the butter over medium heat; add onion and garlic and cook until tender, stirring occasionally. Remove from heat. In a food processor or blender combine half of the onion mixture (reserve the rest in the skillet), the pepper pieces, tomatoes, broth, whipping cream, salt, and black pepper. Cover and process or blend until smooth (mixture will look curdled). Set aside.

3 For filling, add the remaining 1 tablespoon butter and the remaining onion mixture to the skillet. Cook over medium-high heat until butter is melted. Add shrimp and squid; cook and stir for 3 to 4 minutes or just until shrimp is opaque and squid is firm. Remove from heat; stir in parsley. Transfer shrimp mixture to a food processor. Cover and process just until shrimp mixture is finely chopped and mixture starts to come together.

4 Preheat oven to 400°F. Place ham slices on a large cutting board. Top each ham slice with one of the fish fillets. Divide filling among fillets, spreading filling evenly over fillets. Roll up and secure with toothpicks. Place fish rolls, seam sides down, in a 2-quart rectangular baking dish.

5 Bake, covered, for 15 minutes. Uncover and bake for about 10 minutes more or until fish in the center of the rolls flakes when tested with a fork (cut through one of the fish rolls to check center). Meanwhile, place sauce in a small saucepan. Cook over medium heat until heated through, stirring occasionally. Serve sauce with fish rolls.

Nutrition facts per serving: 299 cal., 12 g total fat (6 g. sat fat), 176 mg chol., 707 mg sodium, 10 g carb., 37 g protein.

scallops with GARLICKY TOMATILLO SALSA

Prep: 35 minutes
Chill: 30 minutes
Grill: 2 minutes
Makes: 4 servings

- 8 10- to 12-inch bamboo skewers
- 16 fresh sea scallops (1½ to 2 pounds total)
- 1 tablespoon olive oil
- ½ teaspoon ground ancho chile pepper
- ½ teaspoon smoked paprika
- 1 11- to 12-ounce can tomatillos, rinsed and drained
- ⅓ cup coarsely chopped red onion
- ⅓ cup lightly packed fresh cilantro
- 1 small fresh jalapeño chile pepper, seeded and cut up
- 1 tablespoon lime juice
- 4 large cloves garlic, halved
- ¾ teaspoon ground cumin
- ¼ teaspoon salt
- 4 ounces queso fresco cheese, crumbled (1 cup)

1 Soak bamboo skewers in enough water to cover for 1 hour. Rinse scallops with cold water; pat dry with paper towels. Thread 4 of the scallops onto 2 skewers* that are parallel to each other, leaving ¼ inch between each scallop. Repeat with remaining scallops and skewers to get 4 sets of skewered scallops. Brush scallops with olive oil and sprinkle with ancho chile pepper and smoked paprika. Place on a tray; cover and chill for 30 minutes.

2 Meanwhile, in a food processor or blender combine tomatillos, onion, cilantro, jalapeño pepper, lime juice, garlic, cumin, and salt. Cover and process or blend until consistency of a chunky sauce.

3 For a charcoal grill, place scallops on the rack of an uncovered grill directly over medium-hot coals for 2 to 3 minutes or until scallops are opaque, turning once halfway through grilling. (For a gas grill, preheat grill. Reduce heat to medium-high. Place scallops on grill rack over heat. Cover and grill as above.)

4 To serve, spoon salsa onto serving plates. Top with skewers and sprinkle with cheese.

Nutrition facts per serving: 303 cal., 8 g total fat (2 g sat. fat), 100 mg chol., 1228 mg sodium, 11 g carb., 43 g protein.

*Tip: Threading the scallops onto 2 skewers helps keep them from rolling around and falling off the skewers when grilled.

tomatillo-shrimp
ENCHILADAS

Prep: 30 minutes
Cook: 6 minutes
Bake: 15 minutes
Oven: 375°F
Makes: 8 servings

- 2 **tablespoons olive oil**
- ½ **medium red onion, peeled and thinly sliced**
- ½ **medium green sweet pepper, seeded and thinly sliced**
- 1¼ **pounds medium shrimp, shelled, deveined, and cut in half crossways**
- 1 **cup frozen corn, thawed**
- ¼ **cup water**
- 1 **teaspoon chili powder**
- ½ **teaspoon ground cumin**
- 8 **corn tortillas**
- 1 **16-ounce bottle tomatillo salsa (such as La Victoria)**
- 3 **tablespoons half-and-half**
- 1 **cup shredded reduced-fat Monterey Jack cheese (4 ounces)**

1. Heat oil in a large nonstick skillet over medium-high heat. Add onion and pepper; cook for 3 minutes, stirring occasionally. Add shrimp; cook for an additional 3 minutes, until shrimp is opaque. Stir in corn, the ¼ cup water, chili powder, and cumin. Heat through.

2. Preheat oven to 375°F. Coat a 13×9×2-inch baking dish with nonstick cooking spray.

3. Wrap 4 tortillas in damp paper towels. Microwave for 30 seconds. Brush one side of each tortilla with salsa. Spoon ½ cup shrimp mixture on each. Roll up and place seam-side down in prepared dish. Repeat with remaining tortillas and filling. Top with any extra filling.

4. Mix remaining salsa with half-and-half. Spoon over enchiladas. Sprinkle with cheese. Bake uncovered, for 15 minutes or until bubbly.

Nutrition facts per serving: 240 cal., 8 g total fat (2 g sat. fat), 115 mg chol., 677 mg sodium, 20 g carb., 20 g protein.

spicy shrimp CASSEROLE

Baked tortilla strips make a crunchy topper for this Mexican-seasoned main dish.

Prep: 20 minutes
Bake: 52 minutes
Stand: 10 minutes
Oven: 350°F
Makes: 6 servings

6   6-inch corn tortillas, cut into bite-size strips

1   cup bottled salsa verde

1   cup shredded reduced-fat Monterey Jack cheese (4 ounces)

½   cup light sour cream

3   tablespoons all-purpose flour

¼   cup snipped fresh cilantro

1   12-ounce package frozen cooked, peeled, and deveined shrimp, thawed

1   cup frozen yellow and white whole kernel corn

1   medium tomato, coarsely chopped

¼   cup light sour cream (optional)

1 Preheat oven to 350°F. Place half of the tortilla strips in the bottom of a lightly greased 2-quart baking dish. Arrange remaining tortilla strips on a baking sheet; bake for 12 to 14 minutes or until crisp.

2 Meanwhile, in a large bowl stir together salsa, cheese, the ½ cup sour cream, the flour, and 2 tablespoons of the cilantro. Stir in shrimp and corn. Spoon shrimp mixture over tortilla strips in baking dish.

3 Bake, uncovered, for 40 to 45 minutes or until heated through. Let stand for 10 minutes before serving. Sprinkle with baked tortilla strips, tomato, and the remaining 2 tablespoons cilantro.

4 If desired, serve with the ¼ cup sour cream.

Nutrition facts per serving: 242 cal., 8 g total fat (4 g sat. fat), 129 mg chol., 564 mg sodium, 25 g carb., 20 g protein.

garlic shrimp SKEWERS

Prep: 30 minutes
Marinate: 1 hour
Grill: 8 minutes
Makes: 4 servings

24 fresh or frozen large
   shrimp, peeled and
   deveined

½ cup olive oil

2 tablespoons finely
  chopped fresh cilantro

4 cloves garlic, minced

¼ teaspoon cayenne pepper

3 ounces guava paste,
  cut up

4 teaspoons water

1 canned chipotle chile
  pepper in adobo sauce

2 tablespoons chopped red
  onion

1 small fresh pineapple,
  peeled, cored and cut
  into chunks (2½ cups)
  Coconut Rice*

1 Thaw and rinse shrimp; pat dry with paper towels. Place shrimp in a large resealable plastic bag set in a shallow dish. In a small bowl, combine olive oil, cilantro, garlic, and cayenne. Pour over shrimp; seal bag and marinate in the refrigerator for 1 hour, turning bag occasionally.

2 In a food processor or blender, combine guava paste, water, chipotle, and red onion. Cover and process or blend until almost smooth. Transfer mixture to a large bowl.

3 Using a slotted spoon, remove shrimp from oil mixture and transfer to bowl with guava mixture. Discard remaining oil mixture. Add pineapple to guava mixture. Toss gently to coat pineapple and shrimp with guava mixture. (Do not allow pineapple to stay in mixture for more than 5 minutes or shrimp will become mushy.) Alternately thread shrimp and pineapple on 8 skewers. Reserve remaining guava mixture.

4 For a charcoal grill, grill skewers on the greased rack of an uncovered grill directly over medium heat for 6 to 10 minutes or until shrimp are opaque and pineapple begins to char, turning skewers once halfway through grilling and brushing with reserved guava mixture halfway through grilling. Serve immediately with Coconut Rice.

*Coconut Rice: In a medium saucepan cook and stir 1 cup basmati rice in 1 tablespoon hot butter over medium heat until rice begins to brown. Add 1 cup chicken broth, 1 cup unsweetened coconut milk, and ¼ teaspoon salt. Bring to boiling. Reduce heat and simmer, covered, for 15 minutes or until liquid is absorbed. Stir in ½ cup frozen peas. Cover and let stand 5 minutes. Makes 4 cups.

Nutrition facts per serving: 670 cal., 30 g total fat (14 g sat. fat), 181 mg chol., 628 mg sodium, 71 g carb., 29 g protein.

shrimp TACOS

We used the oven, but you can also heat the tortillas in the skillet after you remove the bean mixture.

Start to Finish: 35 minutes
Makes: 4 (2-taco) servings

- 8 **6-inch corn tortillas**
- 1½ **cups seeded, chopped tomatoes**
- 1 **cup seeded, chopped cucumber**
- ⅓ **cup thinly sliced scallions**
- ¼ **cup chopped fresh cilantro**
- 3 **tablespoons lime juice**
- ¼ **teaspoon salt**
- 8 **ounces green beans, trimmed**
- 1 **teaspoon fajita seasoning**
- 1 **pound medium to large shrimp, peeled and deveined**
- 1 **tablespoon olive oil**

1 Preheat oven to 350°F. Wrap tortillas in foil and heat in oven for 10 minutes. Meanwhile, for salsa combine tomato, cucumber, scallions, cilantro, lime juice and salt; set aside.

2 In a bowl, toss beans with ½ teaspoon of fajita seasoning. In another bowl, toss shrimp with remaining ½ teaspoon seasoning. Heat oil in a large skillet over medium-high heat. Add beans and cook, stirring, for 3 minutes. Add shrimp and stir, cooking for 3 minutes more or until shrimp turn opaque.

3 Divide shrimp-and-bean mixture between warm tortillas. Serve with salsa.

Nutrition facts per serving: 305 cal., 7 g total fat (1 g sat. fat), 172 mg chol., 397 mg sodium, 34 g carb., 28 g protein.

cilantro SHRIMP

Prep: 20 minutes
Grill: 7 minutes
Makes: 4 servings

1 pound fresh or frozen jumbo shrimp in shells (about 20)

2 tablespoons snipped fresh cilantro

1 tablespoon lemon juice

1 tablespoon melted butter

1½ to 2 teaspoons bottled minced garlic

1 fresh red serrano chile pepper, seeded and finely chopped (optional)

1. Thaw shrimp, if frozen. With a sharp paring knife, split each shrimp down the back through the shell, leaving the tails intact; devein shrimp. Flatten shrimp with your hand or the flat side of a knife blade. Rinse shrimp and pat dry with paper towels.

2. For sauce, combine cilantro, lemon juice, butter, garlic, and, if desired, serrano pepper. Place shrimp, split sides down, in a lightly greased grill basket. Brush shrimp with sauce.

3. For a charcoal grill, grill shrimp on the rack of an uncovered grill directly over medium coals for 7 to 9 minutes or until shrimp are opaque, turning basket once halfway through grilling. (For a gas grill, preheat grill. Reduce heat to medium. Place shrimp in basket on grill rack over heat. Cover and grill as above.)

Nutrition facts per serving: 120 cal., 4 g total fat (2 g sat. fat), 137 mg chol., 148 mg sodium, 2 g carb., 18 g protein.

mexican-style SHRIMP PIZZA

Prep: 25 minutes
Bake: 16 minutes
Oven: 400°F
Makes: 4 pizzas

4 8-inch whole wheat flour tortillas

2 teaspoons olive oil

2 large red and/or yellow sweet peppers, seeded and cut into bite-size strips

⅔ cup thinly sliced scallions

1 medium fresh jalapeño chile pepper, seeded and thinly sliced (optional; see tip, page 8)

2 tablespoons water

¼ to ⅓ cup purchased salsa verde

8 ounces peeled and deveined cooked medium shrimp

⅔ cup shredded reduced-fat or regular Monterey Jack cheese

2 tablespoons snipped fresh cilantro

① Preheat oven to 400°F. Brush both sides of each tortilla with oil; place tortillas in a single layer on two ungreased baking sheets. Place sheets on separate oven racks; bake for about 10 minutes or until crisp, turning tortillas and moving baking sheets to opposite racks halfway through baking.

② Meanwhile, coat an unheated large nonstick skillet with nonstick cooking spray. Preheat skillet over medium heat. Add sweet peppers, scallions, and, if desired, chile pepper. Cook for about 5 minutes or until nearly crisp-tender, stirring occasionally. Add the water; cover and cook for 2 minutes more.

③ Spread each tortilla with about 1 tablespoon of the salsa. Top with cooked vegetable mixture and shrimp. Sprinkle with cheese. Bake, one baking sheet at a time, for about 3 minutes or until cheese is melted and shrimp is heated through. Sprinkle with cilantro.

Nutrition facts per pizza: 288 cal., 11 g total fat (4 g sat. fat), 125 mg chol., 673 mg sodium, 22 g carb., 26 g protein.

mexican SHRIMP TOSTADAS

Start to Finish: 20 minutes
Makes: 4 servings

- **4 purchased tostada shells**
- **2 cups shredded lettuce**
- **1 15-ounce can black beans, drained**
- **20 large shrimp, peeled, deveined, cooked, and chilled**
- **1 tablespoon lime juice**
- **1 medium tomato, cut into 16 thin wedges**
- **¼ cup sour cream**
- **Sliced scallions**
- **Salsa**

1 Place one tostada shell on each of four serving plates. Top with some lettuce and ¼ of the beans. Arrange 4 or 5 shrimp in a circle over the beans; sprinkle shrimp with lime juice.

2 Arrange 4 tomato wedges on each tortilla and top with 1 tablespoon of the sour cream and scallions. Serve with some salsa.

Nutrition facts per serving: 273 cal., 6 g total fat (2 g sat. fat), 227 mg chol., 670 mg sodium, 25 g carb., 32 g protein.

beans, rice, & EGGS

Baked Bean and Corn Chimichangas, *page 190*

bean AND CHEESE ENCHILADAS

Prep: 10 minutes
Bake: 15 minutes
Oven: 375°F
Makes: 8 servings

1 **15-ounce can red kidney beans, rinsed and drained**

1 **teaspoon chili powder**

¼ **teaspoon cumin**

¼ **teaspoon salt**

2½ **cups shredded pepper Jack cheese**

1 **10-ounce can hot enchilada sauce**

1 **10-ounce can mild enchilada sauce**

8 **fajita-size flour tortillas (6½-inch)**

1 Preheat oven to 375°F. Mix beans, chili powder, cumin, and salt in bowl. Slightly mash beans; stir to combine. Add 1½ cups cheese.

2 Mix 2 cans enchilada sauce in bowl. Stir 1 cup into bean mixture.

3 Spread ¼ cup sauce mixture in 13×9×2-inch baking dish. Brush one side of a tortilla with sauce. Spoon ¼ cup bean mixture in center on sauced side; roll up; place, seam side down, in dish. Repeat with remaining tortillas and bean mixture. Pour remaining enchilada sauce over top to cover. Top with remaining cheese.

4 Bake for 15 minutes.

Nutrition facts per serving: 352 cal., 23 g total fat (12 g sat. fat), 64 mg chol., 672 mg sodium, 22 g carb., 15 g protein.

bean burritos WITH LIME MAYONNAISE

Start to Finish: 20 minutes
Makes: 4 servings

- 4 **9- to 10-inch flour tortillas**
- 1 **16-ounce can refried beans**
- ¼ **cup salsa**
- ¼ **cup mayonnaise**
- ½ **teaspoon finely shredded lime zest**
- 1 **tablespoon lime juice**
- 2 **cups shredded leaf or iceberg lettuce**
- ½ **cup cherry tomatoes, quartered**
- 2 **ounces Monterey Jack cheese with jalapeño chile peppers, shredded (½ cup)**

1 Place tortillas between paper towels. Microwave on 100 percent power, for 20 to 30 seconds to heat through.

2 Meanwhile, in a small saucepan combine refried beans and salsa. Cook over medium heat until heated through, stirring frequently.

3 In a medium bowl, combine mayonnaise, lime zest, and lime juice. Add lettuce and tomato; toss to coat.

4 Spoon about ½ cup of the bean mixture onto each tortilla just below the center. Top each with 2 tablespoons cheese and about ⅓ cup lettuce mixture. Fold bottom edge of each tortilla up and over the filling. Fold opposite sides in and over filling. Roll up from the bottom.

Nutrition facts per serving: 414 cal., 19 g total fat (6 g sat. fat), 29 mg chol., 992 mg sodium, 47 g carb., 15 g protein.

triple-decker TORTILLA BAKE

Twenty minutes is all it takes to build a healthful family dinner. Salsa, corn, beans, and cheese separate layers of tortillas in this hot Mexican-inspired casserole.

Prep: 20 minutes
Bake: 15 minutes
Oven: 450°F
Makes: 4 servings

- 1 **cup canned pinto beans, rinsed and drained**
- 1 **cup salsa**
- 4 **6-inch corn tortillas**
- ¾ **cup frozen whole kernel corn**
- ½ **cup shredded reduced-fat Monterey Jack cheese or cheddar cheese (2 ounces)**
- ½ **of an avocado, pitted, peeled, and chopped**
- 1 **tablespoon fresh cilantro leaves**

1 Preheat oven to 450°F. Lightly coat a 9-inch pie plate with cooking spray. Place beans in a small bowl; use a fork to slightly mash the beans. In a small saucepan or skillet, cook and stir beans over medium heat for 2 to 3 minutes or until heated through.

2 Spoon ¼ cup of the salsa into bottom of prepared pie plate. Layer ingredients in the following order: one of the tortillas, half of the mashed beans, a second tortilla, all of the corn, ¼ cup of the cheese, ¼ cup of the salsa, a third tortilla, the remaining mashed beans, the remaining tortilla, and the remaining ½ cup salsa.

3 Cover with foil; bake for about 12 minutes or until heated through. Remove foil. Sprinkle with the remaining ¼ cup cheese.

4 Bake, uncovered, for about 3 minutes more or until cheese melts. Top with avocado and cilantro.

Nutrition facts per serving: 221 cal., 7 g total fat (2 g sat. fat), 12 mg chol., 876 mg sodium, 30 g carb., 11 g protein.

grilled black bean AND
SWEET POTATO QUESADILLAS

Prep: 25 minutes
Grill: 7 minutes
Makes: 8 servings

½ **cup chopped onion
(1 medium)**

2 **cloves garlic, minced**

1 **tablespoon olive oil**

1 **15.5-ounce can black
beans, rinsed
and drained**

1 **tablespoon lime juice**

1 **teaspoon dried
oregano, crushed**

1 **teaspoon ground cumin**

4 **10-inch flour tortillas**

1½ **cups mashed cooked
sweet potatoes***

1 **cup shredded Monterey
Jack cheese (4 ounces)**

1½ **cups tightly packed baby
spinach leaves**

½ **to ¾ cup tomato salsa,
corn salsa, and/
or guacamole**

1 In a large skillet, cook onion and garlic in hot oil over medium heat until onion is tender. Stir in black beans, lime juice, oregano, and cumin; heat through.

2 Place one of the tortillas on each of four large plates. Layer one-fourth of the sweet potatoes, 2 tablespoons of the cheese, one-fourth of the bean mixture, one-fourth of the spinach, and another 2 tablespoons of the cheese over half of each tortilla. Fold each tortilla over filling, pressing gently.

3 For a charcoal grill, slide quesadillas from plates onto grill rack directly over low coals. Grill, uncovered, for 3 to 4 minutes or until cheese begins to melt; carefully turn. Grill second side for 4 to 5 minutes or until tortillas are crisp and filling is hot. (For a gas grill, preheat grill. Reduce heat to low. Place quesadillas on the grill rack over heat. Cover and grill as above.)

4 Using a pizza wheel, cut each quesadilla into four wedges. Serve warm with tomato salsa, corn salsa, and/or guacamole.

Nutrition facts per serving: 223 cal., 8 g total fat (3 g sat. fat), 13 mg chol., 484 mg sodium, 32 g carb., 8 g protein.

***Tip:** For the mashed sweet potatoes, wash, peel, and cut off woody portions and ends of about 12 ounces sweet potatoes. Cut sweet potatoes into quarters. In a covered medium saucepan cook sweet potatoes in enough boiling salted water to cover for 25 to 30 minutes or until tender. (Or place in a microwave-safe casserole with ½ cup water. Microwave, covered, on 100 percent power for 8 to 10 minutes or until tender, stirring once.) Drain and mash with a potato masher.

baked bean AND CORN CHIMICHANGAS

Prep: 25 minutes
Bake: 10 minutes
Oven: 425°F
Makes: 6 servings

6   10-inch whole wheat
    flour tortillas

½   cup chopped onion

1   15-ounce can black beans,
    rinsed and drained

1   8.75-ounce can whole
    kernel corn, rinsed
    and drained

1   medium tomato, chopped

1   cup purchased salsa verde
    or red salsa

¼   cup snipped fresh cilantro
    Nonstick cooking spray

3   ounces reduced-fat
    Monterey Jack cheese,
    shredded (¾ cup)

1 Preheat oven to 425°F. Coat a baking sheet with nonstick cooking spray; set aside. Wrap the tortillas in foil. Heat in the oven for 5 minutes.

2 Meanwhile, for the filling, coat an unheated large skillet with nonstick cooking spray. Preheat skillet over medium heat. Add onion; cook for about 5 minutes or until tender, stirring occasionally. Add black beans. Using a fork or potato masher, mash beans slightly. Stir in corn, tomato, and ½ cup of the salsa. Heat through. Stir in cilantro.

3 To assemble, spoon about ½ cup of the filling onto each tortilla, spooning filling just below the center. Fold bottom edge of each tortilla up and over filling. Fold opposite sides in and over filling. Roll up from the bottom. If necessary, secure rolled tortillas with wooden toothpicks. Place filled tortillas on prepared baking sheet, seam sides down. Coat top and sides of the filled tortillas with nonstick cooking spray.

4 Bake for 10 to 12 minutes or until tortillas are golden brown and crisp. To serve, sprinkle chimichangas with cheese and top with the remaining ½ cup salsa.

Nutrition facts per serving: 315 cal., 11 g total fat (3 g sat. fat), 10 mg chol., 1147 mg sodium, 47 g carb., 16 g protein.

tex-mex BEAN TOSTADAS

If you like food fiery hot, use a hot-style salsa. If not, try mild or medium salsa.

Prep: 15 minutes
Bake: 8 minutes
Oven: 350°F
Makes: 4 servings

- **4 packaged tostada shells**
- **1 16-ounce can pinto beans, rinsed and drained**
- **½ cup purchased salsa**
- **½ teaspoon salt-free Southwest chipotle seasoning blend**
- **½ cup shredded reduced-fat cheddar cheese (2 ounces)**
- **1½ cups packaged shredded iceberg lettuce**
- **1 cup chopped tomato (1 large)**
- **¼ cup shredded reduced-fat cheddar cheese (1 ounce; optional)**
- **Lime wedges (optional)**

1 Preheat oven to 350°F. Place tostada shells on a baking sheet. Bake for 3 to 5 minutes or until warm. Meanwhile, in a medium bowl combine beans, salsa, and seasoning blend. Use a potato masher or fork to coarsely mash the mixture. Divide bean mixture among tostada shells, spreading evenly. Top with the ½ cup cheese.

2 Bake for about 5 minutes or until cheese is melted. Top tostadas with shredded lettuce, chopped tomato, and, if desired, the ¼ cup cheese. If desired, serve with lime wedges.

Nutrition facts per serving: 230 cal., 6 g total fat (3 g sat. fat), 10 mg chol., 660 mg sodium, 33 g carb., 12 g protein.

three-bean ENCHILADAS

Prep: 25 minutes
Bake: 25 minutes
Oven: 350°F
Makes: 8 servings

16 6-inch corn tortillas

1 15-ounce can red kidney beans, rinsed and drained

1 15-ounce can pinto beans, rinsed and drained

1 15-ounce can navy beans or Great Northern beans, rinsed and drained

1 10.75-ounce can condensed cheddar cheese soup or nacho cheese soup

1 10-ounce can red or green enchilada sauce

1 8-ounce can tomato sauce

1½ cups shredded Monterey Jack cheese or cheddar cheese (6 ounces)

Sliced pitted black olives (optional)

Chopped green sweet pepper (optional)

1 Preheat oven to 350°F. Stack tortillas and wrap tightly in foil. Bake for about 10 minutes or until warm.

2 For filling, in a large bowl stir together beans and soup. Spoon about ¼ cup of the filling onto one edge of each tortilla. Starting at the edge with the filling, roll up tortilla. Arrange tortillas, seam sides down, in eight ungreased 10- to 12-ounce au gratin dishes or two ungreased 2-quart rectangular baking dishes.

3 For sauce, in a small bowl stir together enchilada sauce and tomato sauce. Spoon over tortillas.

4 Bake, covered, for about 20 minutes for the small dishes (about 30 minutes for the large dishes) or until heated through. Sprinkle with cheese. Bake, uncovered, for about 5 minutes more or until cheese is melted. If desired, sprinkle with olives and sweet pepper.

Nutrition facts per serving: 360 cal., 10 g total fat (5 g sat. fat), 22 mg chol., 1139 mg sodium, 55 g carb., 20 g protein.

frijoles RANCHEROS

Prep: 30 minutes
Cook: 15 minutes
Makes: 8 (½-cup) servings

2 tablespoons vegetable oil

2 medium fresh poblano chile peppers, stemmed, seeded, and chopped (see tip, page 8)

¾ cup chopped onion

2 cloves garlic, minced

8 ounces uncooked chorizo, casings removed if present

2 15-ounce cans pinto beans, rinsed and drained

2 medium tomatoes, chopped

1 cup chicken broth

¼ cup snipped fresh cilantro

½ teaspoon salt

3 tablespoons lime juice

Shredded Monterey Jack cheese or cheddar cheese (optional)

Warmed flour tortillas, corn tortillas, or tortilla chips (optional)

1 In a large skillet, heat oil over medium heat. Add chile peppers, onion, and garlic; cook and stir for 4 to 5 minutes or until tender. Remove onion mixture from skillet; set aside.

2 In the same skillet, cook chorizo over medium heat until cooked through and no longer pink, using a wooden spoon to break up meat as it cooks. Remove chorizo from skillet; drain on paper towels. Return chorizo to skillet.

3 Place beans from one can in a medium bowl. Using a potato masher, mash the beans. Add the mashed beans, whole beans from remaining can, and the onion mixture to chorizo in skillet. Stir to combine.

4 Stir in tomatoes, broth, cilantro, and salt. Bring to boiling; reduce heat. Simmer, uncovered, for about 15 minutes or until slightly thickened, stirring occasionally. Remove from heat. Stir in lime juice.

5 If desired, top with cheese and serve with warmed tortillas.

Nutrition facts per serving: 279 cal., 15 g total fat (4 g sat. fat), 25 mg chol., 961 mg sodium, 24 g carb., 15 g protein.

crispy bean AND CHEESE BURRITOS

Prep: 10 minutes
Cook: 18 minutes
Makes: 6 servings

1 3.5-ounce bag boil-in-bag brown rice

1 cup salsa

⅓ cup chopped fresh cilantro

1 avocado, pitted, peeled, and cut into ½-inch pieces

1 tablespoon lime juice

6 soft taco-size flour tortillas

1 cup shredded pepper Jack cheese (4 ounces)

1 15.5-ounce can black beans, rinsed and drained

  Nonstick cooking spray

1 Prepare rice according to package directions. Drain and place in a medium bowl. Stir in salsa and cilantro. In a small bowl, gently stir together avocado pieces with lime juice.

2 Place tortillas on work surface and sprinkle 2 tablespoons cheese in center of each, from left to right. Top cheese with a heaping ¼ cup black beans. Place a heaping ⅓ cup rice mixture over beans, then divide avocado pieces among tortillas. Fold up tortillas like an envelope.

3 Heat a large nonstick skillet over medium-high heat. Coat top and bottom of burritos with nonstick cooking spray. Place 3 burritos in skillet, seam-side down; cook for 1 to 2 minutes or until lightly browned and crisp. Turn burritos over and cook for another 2 minutes. Repeat with remaining burritos, reducing heat if they get too browned.

Nutrition facts per serving: 415 cal., 15 g total fat (4 g sat. fat), 17 mg chol., 761 mg sodium, 54 g carb., 15 g protein.

mexican RED RICE

Prep: 20 minutes
Cook: 20 minutes
Stand: 5 minutes
Makes: about 4 cups

1 **tablespoon vegetable oil**
½ **cup chopped onion
(1 medium)**
2 **cloves garlic, minced**
1 **teaspoon ground ancho
chile pepper**
¼ **teaspoon kosher salt**
1 **cup long grain rice**
1 **14-ounce can reduced-
sodium chicken broth or
vegetable broth**
¾ **cup purchased salsa**
¼ **cup water**
½ **cup finely snipped
fresh cilantro**

1 In a medium saucepan, heat oil over medium-high heat. Add onion, garlic, ground ancho chile pepper, and salt; cook for 2 minutes. Stir in uncooked rice; cook and stir for 1 minute. Add broth, salsa, and the water. Bring to boiling; reduce heat. Simmer, covered, for about 20 minutes or until rice is tender.

2 Remove pan from heat. Remove lid. Cover pan with a clean kitchen towel; replace lid. Let stand for 5 minutes to let the towel absorb any excess moisture. Remove lid and towel. Add cilantro; fluff rice with a fork.

Nutrition facts per ⅔ cup: 166 cal., 4 g total fat (0 g sat. fat), 0 mg chol., 323 mg sodium, 29 g carb., 4 g protein.

mexican GREEN RICE

Prep: 20 minutes
Cook: 20 minutes
Stand: 5 minutes
Makes: 3½ cups

- 1 **tablespoon vegetable oil**
- ½ **cup chopped onion (1 medium)**
- 2 **cloves garlic, minced**
- ½ **teaspoon kosher salt**
- 1 **cup reduced-sodium chicken broth or vegetable broth**
- ¾ **cup purchased salsa verde**
- 1 **cup long grain white rice**
- ½ **cup finely snipped fresh cilantro**

1 In a medium saucepan, heat oil over medium-high heat. Add onion, garlic, and salt; cook for about 2 minutes or until onion is tender. Stir in broth and salsa; bring to boiling. Stir in uncooked rice; reduce heat. Simmer, covered, for 20 to 30 minutes or until tender.

2 Remove pan from heat. Remove lid. Cover pan with a clean kitchen towel; replace lid. Let stand for 5 minutes to let the towel absorb any excess moisture. Remove lid and towel. Add cilantro; fluff rice with a fork.

Nutrition facts per ½ cup: 143 cal., 3 g total fat (0 g sat. fat), 0 mg chol., 242 mg sodium, 25 g carb., 3 g protein.

oaxacan rice AND BEANS

In most of southern Mexico, black beans are more popular than pinto beans. In this recipe, they're cooked with rice and two kinds of chiles—the mild poblano and the fiery serrano.

Prep: 30 minutes
Cook: 20 minutes
Makes: about 5½ cups
(6 side-dish or
3 or 4 main-dish
servings)

½ cup finely chopped carrot

½ cup chopped onion
(1 medium)

1 fresh poblano chile
pepper, stemmed,
seeded, and finely
chopped, (see tip, page
8), or one 4-ounce can
chopped green chile
peppers, drained

1 fresh serrano or jalapeño
chile pepper, stemmed,
seeded, and finely
chopped, (see tip, page
8), or 1 canned jalapeño
chile pepper, rinsed,
drained, seeded, and
finely chopped (see tip,
page 8)

2 cloves garlic, minced

1 tablespoon vegetable oil

1 cup long grain white rice

2¼ cups chicken broth or
vegetable broth

¼ teaspoon salt

1 cup frozen cut green
beans, thawed

1 15-ounce can black beans,
rinsed and drained

1 In a large skillet, cook carrot, onion, poblano pepper, serrano pepper, and garlic in hot oil for 3 minutes. Stir in uncooked rice. Cook and stir constantly over medium heat for 2 to 3 minutes or until rice is lightly browned.

2 Carefully stir in broth and salt. Bring to boiling; reduce heat. Simmer, covered, for 15 minutes. Add green beans; cover and cook for about 5 minutes more or until rice is tender and liquid is absorbed. Stir in black beans; heat through.

Nutrition facts per serving: 208 cal., 3 g total fat (1 g sat. fat), 1 mg chol., 643 mg sodium, 40 g carb., 8 g protein.

spicy rice AND
BEAN CAKES

Prep: 30 minutes
Cook: 8 minutes per batch
Makes: 4 servings

1 medium red sweet
   pepper, seeded and
   finely chopped

2 cloves garlic, minced

1 15-ounce can black beans,
   rinsed and drained

1½ cups cooked brown rice

1 egg, lightly beaten

2 tablespoons snipped
   fresh cilantro

1 canned chipotle chile
   pepper in adobo sauce,
   finely chopped (see tip,
   page 8)

1 teaspoon adobo sauce
   from canned chipotle
   chile peppers in adobo
   sauce (optional)

½ teaspoon ground cumin

4 teaspoons olive oil

¼ cup light sour cream
   Snipped fresh cilantro
   (optional)

1 Coat an unheated large nonstick skillet with nonstick cooking spray. Preheat over medium-high heat. Add sweet pepper and garlic; cook and stir until crisp-tender. Transfer to a large bowl and cool slightly.

2 Place black beans in a food processor;* cover and process until smooth. Transfer to bowl with sweet pepper mixture. Stir in cooked brown rice, egg, the 2 tablespoons cilantro, the chipotle pepper, adobo sauce (if using), and cumin; mix well. With wet hands, shape mixture evenly into 8 patties, each about ½ inch thick.

3 In the same skillet, heat 2 teaspoons of the olive oil over medium heat. Add half of the bean patties. Cook for 8 to 10 minutes or until browned and heated through, carefully turning once halfway through cooking. Remove from skillet and keep warm. Repeat with remaining 2 teaspoons oil and remaining bean patties. Serve bean patties with sour cream. If desired, garnish with additional snipped cilantro.

Nutrition facts per serving: 236 cal., 8 g total fat (2 g sat. fat), 57 mg chol., 307 mg sodium, 35 g carb., 11 g protein.

*Tip: If you do not have a food processor, use a potato masher to mash the beans into a nearly smooth paste.

seafood omelet WITH AVOCADO SALSA

Start to Finish: 20 minutes
Makes: 4 servings

- 1 **medium avocado, pitted, peeled, and chopped**
- 1 **tablespoon finely chopped red onion**
- 1 **tablespoon snipped fresh cilantro**
- 1 **tablespoon lime juice**
  Salt and ground black pepper
- 8 **eggs**
- ½ **cup water**
- ¼ **cup chopped scallions**
- ¼ **teaspoon salt**
- ¼ **teaspoon ground black pepper**
- ¼ **teaspoon cayenne pepper**
- 4 **tablespoons butter**
- 8 **ounces cooked crab leg meat**

1 For avocado salsa, in a medium bowl combine avocado, red onion, cilantro, and lime juice. Season to taste with salt and black pepper. Set aside.

2 In a large bowl, combine eggs, the water, scallions, the ¼ teaspoon salt, the ¼ teaspoon black pepper, and the cayenne. Beat with a fork until combined but not frothy. Heat an 8-inch nonstick skillet with flared sides over medium-high heat until skillet is hot.

3 Add 1 tablespoon of the butter to the hot skillet. When butter melts, add ½ cup of the egg mixture; lower heat to medium. Immediately begin stirring the eggs gently but continuously with a wooden or plastic spatula until mixture resembles small pieces of cooked egg surrounded by liquid egg. Stop stirring. Cook for 30 to 60 seconds more or until egg mixture is set and shiny.

4 Spoon one-fourth of the crabmeat across center of eggs. With a spatula, lift and fold an edge of the omelet about a third of the way toward the center. Remove from heat. Fold the opposite edge toward the center; transfer to a warm plate. Repeat with the remaining butter, egg mixture, and crabmeat to make four omelets. Serve immediately with avocado salsa.

Nutrition facts per serving: 373 cal., 29 g total fat (10 g sat. fat), 493 mg chol., 665 mg sodium, 6 g carb., 22 g protein.

mexican sausage STRATA

To lower the sodium in this cheesy, make-ahead breakfast dish, use ground turkey instead of the breakfast sausage; add an herb such as thyme or oregano.

Prep: 25 minutes
Bake: 35 minutes
Stand: 5 minutes
Oven: 325°F
Makes: 6 servings

5 slices white or whole wheat bread, cubed (3¾ cups)

6 ounces ground turkey sausage

3 eggs

1 cup skim milk

½ cup light sour cream

½ cup shredded Monterey Jack cheese with jalapeño chile peppers (2 ounces)

⅓ cup shredded reduced-fat sharp cheddar cheese

⅓ cup salsa

1 Coat a 9- or 10-inch quiche dish with nonstick cooking spray. Spread bread cubes evenly in the quiche dish.

2 Crumble turkey sausage into a medium skillet; cook until brown. Drain off fat. Pat with paper towels to remove excess fat. Sprinkle cooked sausage over bread cubes in quiche dish.

3 In a medium mixing bowl, beat together eggs, milk, and sour cream. Stir in Monterey Jack and cheddar cheeses. Pour egg mixture over sausage in quiche dish. Cover and refrigerate for at least 2 hours.

4 Preheat oven to 325°F. Uncover and bake for 35 to 40 minutes or until center is set and top is golden brown. Remove from oven. Let stand for 5 to 10 minutes before cutting. To serve, cut strata into wedges. Spoon some salsa on top of each serving.

Nutrition facts per serving: 254 cal., 13 g total fat (6 g sat. fat), 134 mg chol., 556 mg sodium, 17 g carb., 18 g protein.

Make-Ahead Directions: Assemble strata. Cover and refrigerate for up to 24 hours before baking as directed above.

breakfast MIGAS

Prep: 25 minutes
Cook: 5 to 6 hours (low)
Makes: 6 servings

**Disposable slow
cooker liner**

1 **pound bulk breakfast
sausage, browned
and drained**

1 **4.5-ounce package
tostada shells,
coarsely broken**

¾ **cup chopped red sweet
pepper (1 medium)**

½ **cup chopped onion
(1 medium)**

1 **4-ounce can diced
green chile peppers**

12 **eggs, or 3½ cups
refrigerated or frozen
egg product**

1 **10.75-ounce can
condensed nacho cheese
soup**

¼ **teaspoon ground black
pepper**

2 **avocados, pitted, peeled,
and chopped**

2 **cups refrigerated
fresh salsa**

1 **8-ounce carton
sour cream**

1 Line a 3½ or 4-quart slow cooker with a disposable slow cooker liner. In a very large bowl, combine sausage, broken tostada shells, sweet pepper, onion, and undrained diced green chiles. In a large bowl, whisk together eggs, soup, and pepper. Pour over sausage mixture; transfer to prepared slow cooker.

2 Cover and cook on low-heat setting for 5 to 6 hours. Serve with avocados, salsa, and sour cream.

Nutrition facts per serving: 591 cal., 37 g total fat (13 g sat. fat), 482 mg chol., 1578 mg sodium, 33 g carb., 31 g protein.

scrambled EGG MOLLETES

Prep: 30 minutes
Broil: 3 minutes
Makes: 6 servings

3 bolillos (Mexican rolls) or large crusty hard rolls

2 tablespoons butter, melted

3 ounces uncooked chorizo sausage, casings removed if present

½ of a 16-ounce can refried beans (about 1 cup)

8 eggs

2 tablespoons milk

½ teaspoon chili powder
  Pinch salt

1 tablespoon butter

1 medium avocado, pitted, peeled, and sliced

3 ounces queso Chihuahua or Monterey Jack cheese, shredded (¾ cup)

¾ cup purchased salsa (optional)

1 Preheat broiler. Slice each roll in half horizontally. Brush each cut side of rolls with some of the 2 tablespoons butter. Place rolls, cut sides up, on a baking sheet. Broil 5 inches from the heat for 1 to 2 minutes or until golden brown; set aside.

2 In a large skillet, cook chorizo over medium heat until brown, using a wooden spoon to break up meat as it cooks. Drain well on paper towels; set aside.

3 Spoon refried beans into a small microwave-safe bowl. Microwave on 100 percent power for about 1½ minutes or until heated through, stirring once.

4 In a medium bowl, combine eggs, milk, chili powder, and salt. Beat lightly with a fork. In a large nonstick skillet, melt the 1 tablespoon butter over medium heat. Add egg mixture and chorizo; cook for 2 to 3 minutes or until egg mixture is cooked through but still glossy and moist, lifting and folding the mixture with a spatula as needed while cooking.

5 Spoon refried beans on the cut sides of the roll halves; spread beans evenly. Place roll halves on a baking sheet. Top beans with scrambled eggs, avocado slices, and cheese. Broil 5 inches from the heat for about 3 minutes or just until cheese is melted and bubbly.

6 If desired, serve molletes with salsa.

Nutrition facts per serving: 438 cal., 27 g total fat (11 g sat. fat), 325 mg chol., 713 mg sodium, 29 g carb., 21 g protein.

easy huevos RANCHEROS CASSEROLE

Prep: 15 minutes
Bake: 38 minutes
Stand: 10 minutes
Oven: 375°F
Makes: 12 servings

1 32-ounce package frozen fried potato nuggets

12 eggs

1 cup milk

1½ teaspoons dried oregano, crushed

1½ teaspoons ground cumin

½ teaspoon chili powder

¼ teaspoon garlic powder

1 8-ounce package shredded Mexican cheese blend (2 cups)

1 16-ounce jar thick and chunky salsa

1 8-ounce carton sour cream

1 Preheat oven to 375°F. Lightly coat a 3-quart rectangular baking dish with cooking spray. Arrange frozen potato nuggets in dish.

2 In a large bowl, whisk together eggs, milk, oregano, cumin, chili powder, and garlic powder. Pour egg mixture over potato nuggets.

3 Bake for 35 to 40 minutes or until a knife inserted near the center comes out clean. Sprinkle cheese over egg mixture. Bake for about 3 minutes more or until cheese melts. Let stand for 10 minutes before serving. Serve with salsa and sour cream.

Nutrition facts per serving: 343 cal., 21 g total fat (9 g sat. fat), 238 mg chol., 823 mg sodium, 26 g carb., 14 g protein.

tortilla scramble WITH FRESH SALSA

Chilaquiles (chee-lah-KEE-lehs), a Mexican dish of tortillas simmered in a spicy tomato sauce, inspired this scramble.

Start to Finish: 35 minutes
Makes: 4 servings

- 1 tablespoon butter
- ½ cup snipped fresh cilantro
- 1 small bunch scallions, chopped
- 1 10-ounce can purchased enchilada sauce
- 5 cups yellow corn tortilla chips
- 6 eggs, lightly beaten
- ¼ cup milk
- Salt and ground black pepper
- Fresh Salsa*
- Sour cream (optional)
- Farmer cheese (optional)
- Lime wedges

1 Heat 1 teaspoon of the butter in a 12-inch skillet over medium heat; add half of the cilantro and half of the scallions (use remaining for Fresh Salsa). Cook and stir for 1 minute. Stir in enchilada sauce; gently stir in chips. Cook and stir until chips are coated in sauce; reduce heat to low.

2 For scrambled eggs, in medium bowl whisk together eggs, milk, and ¼ teaspoon each salt and pepper. In large skillet, melt remaining 2 teaspoons butter over medium heat; add eggs. With spatula, lift and fold partially cooked egg mixture from edges to center so that the uncooked egg portion flows underneath. Continue for 4 to 5 minutes or until eggs are cooked through, but still glossy and moist. Remove from heat.

3 To serve, slide chip mixture onto large platter. Top with eggs and Fresh Salsa. Serve with sour cream, cheese, and lime wedges.

*Fresh Salsa: In bowl combine the reserved cilantro and scallions; 1 cup grape tomatoes, halved; 1 avocado, peeled, pitted, and chopped; 1 serrano pepper (see tip, page 8), seeded and chopped; and the juice from half a lime. Cut remaining lime half into wedges for serving.

Nutrition facts per serving: 382 cal., 24 g total fat (6 g sat. fat), 326 mg chol., 874 mg sodium, 32 g carb., 14 g protein.

casserole-style CHILES RELLENOS

This is a streamlined version of the classic Mexican dish chiles rellenos. Filled with gooey cheese and mild peppers, it's great for dinner or brunch.

Prep: 25 minutes
Bake: 17 minutes
Stand: 5 minutes
Oven: 450°F
Makes: 8 servings

- **4** large fresh poblano chile peppers or green sweet peppers (1 pound; see tip, page 8)
- **2** cups shredded Monterey Jack cheese with jalapeño chile peppers (8 ounces)
- **6** eggs, beaten
- **½** cup milk
- **⅔** cup all-purpose flour
- **1** teaspoon baking powder
- **½** teaspoon ground red pepper
- **¼** teaspoon salt
- **1½** cups shredded cheddar cheese (6 ounces)
- **1** cup purchased picante sauce
- **½** cup sour cream

1 Preheat oven to 450°F. Quarter the peppers and remove stems, seeds, and veins. Immerse peppers in boiling water for 3 minutes. Drain. Invert peppers on paper towels to drain well. Place the peppers, cut sides up, in a well-greased 3-quart square baking dish. Top with Monterey Jack cheese.

2 In a medium bowl, whisk together eggs and milk. Add flour, baking powder, red pepper, and salt. Whisk until smooth. Pour egg mixture over peppers and cheese in dish.

3 Bake, uncovered, for 15 to 20 minutes or until a knife inserted near the center comes out clean. Sprinkle with cheddar cheese. Bake for 2 to 3 minutes more or until cheese melts. Let stand for 5 minutes. Serve with picante sauce and sour cream.

Nutrition facts per serving: 347 cal., 23 g total fat (13 g sat. fat), 212 mg chol., 706 mg sodium, 16 g carb., 20 g protein.

To Tote: Do not let stand after baking. Cover tightly. Transport in an insulated carrier. Transport picante sauce and sour cream in tightly covered containers in a separate insulated carrier.

desserts

Ancho Chile Truffles, *page 214*

ancho chile TRUFFLES

Prep: 45 minutes
Chill: 2 hours
Stand: 2 hours
Makes: about 30 truffles

1½ **cups whipping cream**

1 **tablespoon ground ancho chile pepper**

1 **tablespoon ground cinnamon**

¾ **teaspoon cayenne pepper**

½ **teaspoon salt**

1 **pound bittersweet chocolate, chopped into ½-inch pieces**

2 **cups unsweetened Dutch-process cocoa powder**

1½ **teaspoons ground ancho chile pepper**

1 In a medium saucepan combine whipping cream, the 1 tablespoon ancho chile pepper, cinnamon, cayenne pepper, and salt. Bring to boiling. Remove from heat; cover saucepan and let mixture stand for 2 hours.

2 Reheat cream mixture over medium heat just until boiling. Add chocolate pieces. Let stand for 5 minutes. Stir until chocolate is melted and mixture is perfectly smooth.

3 Pour chocolate mixture into a parchment- or waxed paper-lined 13x9-inch baking pan. Chill for 2 to 4 hours or until set.

4 Using a 1-inch scoop or a measuring tablespoon, scoop chocolate mixture into balls (about 30 balls). Quickly roll balls between palms of your hands to smooth the surface. Place on waxed paper. If necessary, chill for 5 to 10 minutes to set up.

5 In a small bowl combine cocoa powder and the 1½ teaspoons ancho chile pepper. Roll balls in cocoa mixture to coat well. Place balls on a parchment- or waxed paper-lined baking sheet and chill until serving time, up to 2 hours.* If chilled longer than 30 minutes, let stand at room temperature for 30 minutes before serving.

Nutrition facts per truffle: 132 cal., 11 g total fat (7 g sat. fat), 17 mg chol., 49 mg sodium, 12 g carb., 2 g protein.

Make-Ahead Directions: Store, tightly covered, in the refrigerator for up to 2 weeks.

chocolate pudding WEDGES
WITH CINNAMON TOASTS

Prep: 45 minutes
Cool: 2 hours
Broil: 2 minutes
Makes: 12 servings

⅔ **cup natural unsweetened cocoa powder**

¼ **cup granulated sugar**

¼ **cup cornstarch**

¼ **teaspoon salt**

3 **cups whole milk**

½ **cup whipping cream**

10 **ounces bittersweet chocolate (60 to 62% cacao), chopped**

2 **tablespoons dark rum (optional)**

2 **teaspoons vanilla extract**

¼ **cup packed brown sugar**

2 **tablespoons unsalted butter, melted**

1 **teaspoon ground cinnamon**

⅛ **teaspoon salt**

12 **¾-inch-thick baguette slices**

Natural unsweetened cocoa powder

Dark grapes (optional)

1 In large heavy saucepan, whisk cocoa powder, granulated sugar, cornstarch, and ¼ teaspoon salt. Add ½ cup of the milk; whisk to a smooth paste. Whisk in remaining milk and whipping cream. Stir constantly over medium heat until pudding thickens and begins to bubble at edges. Stir 30 seconds more. Add chocolate; stir for 1 minute to melt. Remove from heat; stir in rum and vanilla.

2 Transfer pudding to lightly oiled 9-inch deep-dish pie plate. Cool, uncovered, for 2 hours at room temperature. Cover and refrigerate overnight.

3 For cinnamon toasts, in small bowl combine brown sugar, butter, cinnamon, and ⅛ teaspoon salt. Spread on one side of each baguette slice. Place on baking sheet. Broil 5 to 6 inches from heat for 2 to 3 minutes or until toasted and sugar mixture is bubbly.

4 Sprinkle pudding with additional cocoa powder. To serve, cut in wedges or, with a large spoon, spoon in free-form wedges. Serve with cinnamon toasts and grapes.

Nutrition facts per serving: 310 cal., 18 g total fat (11 g sat. fat), 25 mg chol., 208 mg sodium, 39 g carb., 6 g protein.

grilled peaches WITH HONEY AND QUESO FRESCO

Prep: 15 minutes
Grill: 6 minutes
Makes: 6 servings

½ **cup honey**

1 **tablespoon white wine vinegar**

½ **teaspoon ground ancho chile pepper**

1 **teaspoon finely snipped fresh sage**

6 **ripe peaches**

4 **ounces queso fresco, coarsely crumbled (1 cup)**

Fresh sage sprigs (optional)

1 In a small saucepan, combine honey, vinegar, ancho chile pepper, and snipped sage. Heat and stir over medium heat just until mixture comes to boiling. Remove from heat; cool slightly.

2 Cut peaches in half lengthwise; remove pits. Brush cut sides of peaches using the honey mixture.

3 For a charcoal grill, grill peach halves, cut sides down, on the rack of an uncovered grill directly over medium coals for 6 to 8 minutes or until lightly browned and warmed through, turning once halfway through grilling. (For a gas grill, preheat grill. Reduce heat to medium. Place peach halves on grill rack over heat. Cover and grill as above.)

4 Place two peach halves on each of six dessert plates. Evenly drizzle the remaining honey mixture on top of peaches; sprinkle with queso fresco. If desired, garnish with sage sprigs. Serve warm.

Nutrition facts per serving: 181 cal., 1 g total fat (0 g sat. fat), 0 mg chol., 4 mg sodium, 39 g carb., 6 g protein.

mexican CHOCOLATE ICE CREAM

Chocolate syrup, as well as cinnamon and almond extract, lend a Mexican accent to this cool-and-creamy treat.

Prep: 20 minutes
Chill: 6 hours
Freeze: per manufacturer's directions
Cool: 4 hours
Makes: 3½ quarts

- 3 **eggs**
- ½ **cup sugar**
- 6 **cups half-and-half or light cream**
- 1 **16-ounce can chocolate-flavor syrup**
- 1 **tablespoon vanilla extract**
- ½ **teaspoon ground cinnamon**
- ¼ **teaspoon almond extract**
- 2 **cups whipping cream**

1 In a medium bowl, beat eggs with an electric mixer on medium speed until frothy. Add sugar and beat until thick.

2 In a Dutch oven, heat half-and-half until almost boiling. Stir 1 cup of the hot half-and-half into the egg mixture; return all to the Dutch oven. Cook and stir for about 3 minutes or just until mixture comes to a boil (watch carefully because mixture will foam).

3 Remove from heat; strain mixture through a fine-mesh sieve. Stir chocolate-flavor syrup, vanilla, cinnamon, and almond extract into strained mixture. Set mixture aside to cool slightly. Cover and chill for 6 to 24 hours.

4 Stir in whipping cream. Freeze in a 4- or 5-quart ice cream freezer according to manufacturer's directions. Ripen about 4 hours before serving.*

Nutrition facts per ½-cup serving: 191 cal., 13 g total fat (8 g sat. fat), 65 mg chol., 41 mg sodium, 17 g carb., 3 g protein.

When using an ice cream freezer with an insulated freezer bowl, transfer the ice cream to a covered freezer container and ripen by freezing in your regular freezer for about 4 hours (or check the manufacturer's recommendations).

*Tip: Ripening homemade ice cream improves the texture and helps keep it from melting too quickly during eating. To ripen in a traditional-style ice cream freezer, after churning, remove the lid and dasher and cover the top of the freezer can with waxed paper or foil. Plug the hole in the lid with a small piece of cloth; replace lid. Pack outer freezer bucket with enough ice and rock salt to cover top of freezer can (use 1 cup salt for each 4 cups ice). Ripen about 4 hours.

toasted coconut ICE CREAM

Prep: 25 minutes
Chill: 6 hours
Freeze: per manufacturer's
directions
Makes: 12 servings

2 **12-ounce cans
   evaporated milk**

1 **cup unsweetened
   coconut milk**

1 **cup sugar**

2 **cups whipping cream**

1 **tablespoon lemon juice or
   lime juice**

1 **tablespoon vanilla extract**

1⅔ **cups coconut, toasted**

1 In a large bowl, combine evaporated milk, coconut milk, and sugar. Stir until sugar dissolves. Stir in whipping cream, lemon juice, and vanilla. Stir in 1⅓ cups of the toasted coconut.

2 Freeze in a 2-quart ice cream freezer according to the manufacturer's directions. If desired, ripen for 4 hours.*

3 To serve, spoon ice cream into serving dishes; sprinkle with remaining ⅓ cup toasted coconut.

Nutrition facts per serving: 449 cal., 26 g total fat (18 g sat. fat), 71 mg chol., 84 mg sodium, 48 g carb., 6 g protein.

When using an ice cream freezer with an insulated freezer bowl, transfer the ice cream to a covered freezer container and ripen by freezing in your regular freezer for about 4 hours (or check the manufacturer's recommendations).

*****Tip:** Ripening homemade ice cream improves the texture and helps keep it from melting too quickly during eating. To ripen in a traditional-style ice cream freezer, after churning, remove the lid and dasher and cover the top of the freezer can with waxed paper or foil. Plug the hole in the lid with a small piece of cloth; replace lid. Pack outer freezer bucket with enough ice and rock salt to cover top of freezer can (use 1 cup salt for each 4 cups ice). Ripen for about 4 hours.

chocolate-ancho CRÈME BRÛLÉE

Prep: 25 minutes
Bake: 35 minutes
Chill: 1 hour
Oven: 325°F
Makes: 6 servings

2 **cups half-and-half or light cream**

1 **3-inch stick cinnamon**

4 **ounces bittersweet or semisweet chocolate, chopped**

5 **egg yolks, lightly beaten**

⅓ **cup sugar**

1 **teaspoon vanilla extract**

½ **teaspoon ground ancho chile pepper**

⅛ **teaspoon salt**

2 **tablespoons sugar**

¼ **teaspoon ground cinnamon**

1 Preheat oven to 325°F. In a heavy small saucepan, heat half-and-half and cinnamon stick over medium heat just until bubbly. Remove from heat; remove cinnamon stick. Add chocolate to cream. Let stand for 5 minutes; whisk until smooth.

2 Meanwhile, in a medium bowl combine egg yolks, ⅓ cup sugar, the vanilla, chile pepper, and salt. Whisk until combined. Slowly whisk the chocolate mixture into the egg mixture.

3 Place six 5- to 6-ounce ungreased casseroles, soufflé dishes, or custard cups in a 13×9×2-inch baking dish or pan. Divide custard mixture mixture evenly among the soufflé dishes. Place baking dish on oven rack. Pour enough boiling water into the baking dish to reach halfway up the sides of the casseroles.

4 Bake for 35 to 40 minutes or until a knife inserted near the centers comes out clean. Carefully remove casseroles from water; cool on a wire rack. Cover and chill for at least 1 hour or up to 24 hours.

5 Before serving, let custards stand at room temperature for 20 minutes.

6 In a small bowl, combine 2 tablespoons sugar and the ground cinnamon. Sprinkle evenly atop custards. Place on a baking sheet. Caramelize sugar with a culinary torch or broil 4 to 5 inches from heat for 1 to 2 minutes until sugar is melted and lightly browned. Serve immediately.

Nutrition facts per serving: 307 cal., 20 g total fat (11 g sat. fat), 205 mg chol., 91 mg sodium, 30 g carb., 6 g protein.

banana-caramel CUSTARD

Prep: 40 minutes
Bake: 1¼ hours
Cool: 2¼ hours
Oven: 350°F
Makes: 10 to 12 servings

1½ cups sugar

3 cups eggnog

6 eggs

2 teaspoons vanilla extract

⅛ teaspoon salt

2 tablespoons butter

⅛ teaspoon ground cinnamon

1 to 2 ripe but firm bananas, sliced ¼ to ½ inch thick

1 Preheat oven to 350°F. Place rack in center of oven.

2 In a heavy 10-inch skillet, heat ½ cup of the sugar over medium-high heat until sugar begins to melt, shaking the skillet occasionally for even melting. Do not stir. When sugar starts to melt, reduce heat to low; cook for about 5 minutes more or until all sugar is melted and golden brown, stirring with a wooden spoon. Immediately pour caramelized sugar into a 10-cup soufflé dish;* tilt to coat the entire bottom of the dish.

3 In a large bowl, whisk together the remaining 1 cup sugar, the eggnog, eggs, vanilla, and salt until well combined. Pour eggnog mixture into the prepared soufflé dish. Place dish in a large, deep roasting pan. Place roasting pan on rack in oven. Pour boiling water into the roasting pan around dish to a depth of 2 inches.

4 Bake for about 1¼ hours or until a knife inserted near the center comes out clean (custard will not appear set when gently shaken). Cool custard in roasting pan on a wire rack for 15 minutes. Remove dish from roasting pan. Cool on a wire rack for 2 hours. Cover and chill overnight or for up to 2 days.

5 Just before serving, run a thin metal spatula or sharp knife around edges of custard in dish. Invert a serving plate over dish; turn dish and plate over together. Remove dish.

6 In a large skillet, melt butter. Stir in cinnamon. Add banana slices. Cook for 4 to 6 minutes or until golden, turning slices once halfway through cooking. Arrange bananas over custard on serving plate. Spoon some of the caramel sauce over the bananas.

Nutrition facts per serving: 296 cal., 11 g total fat (6 g sat. fat), 178 mg chol., 129 mg sodium, 44 g carb., 7 g protein.

capirotada

Unlike other bread puddings, Mexican-style bread pudding includes plantains, almonds, and Mexican cheese, and it's finished with a tangy cream sauce.

Prep: 30 minutes
Bake: 35 minutes
Oven: 350°F
Makes: 6 to 8 servings

2 cups torn firm-texture bread or French bread

¾ cup water

½ cup packed brown sugar

1 3-inch cinnamon stick

2 whole cloves

2 apples, peeled, cored, and sliced

1 ripe medium plantain or firm large banana, peeled and sliced

⅓ cup golden raisins

¼ cup coarsely chopped almonds, toasted

½ cup shredded asadero, Chihuahua, or Monterey Jack cheese (2 ounces; optional)

Mexican crema, crème fraîche, or sour cream

1 Preheat oven to 350°F. To dry bread, place bread pieces on a baking sheet. Bake for 8 to 10 minutes or until dried.

2 Meanwhile, for syrup, in a small saucepan combine the water, brown sugar, stick cinnamon, and cloves. Bring to boiling; reduce heat. Boil gently, uncovered, for 8 to 10 minutes or until syrup is reduced to ¾ cup. Using a slotted spoon, remove spices and discard.

3 In a large bowl, toss together dried bread pieces and syrup. Add sliced apples, sliced plantain, raisins, and almonds; toss gently. Transfer mixture to an ungreased 2-quart baking dish.

4 Bake, covered, for 35 to 40 minutes or until apples are tender. Remove from oven. If desired, sprinkle with cheese. Serve warm with crema.

Nutrition facts per serving: 212 cal., 2 g total fat (0 g sat. fat), 0 mg chol., 54 mg sodium, 47 g carb., 3 g protein.

chocolate NACHOS

If you like your chocolate soft and gooey, serve these immediately after drizzling. If you prefer it firmer, let the nachos cool for 10 to 15 minutes.

Start to Finish: 35 minutes
Oven: 350°F
Makes: 64 wedges

¼ **cup sugar**

¼ **teaspoon ground cinnamon**

8 **6-inch flour tortillas**

¼ **cup butter (no substitutes), melted**

1 **cup semisweet chocolate pieces**

2 **teaspoons shortening**

1 Preheat oven to 350°F. Combine sugar and cinnamon in a small bowl. Brush one side of each tortilla with melted butter; sprinkle with sugar mixture. Cut each tortilla into 8 wedges. Arrange half of the wedges in a single layer on a 15×10×1-inch baking pan. Bake for 10 to 12 minutes or until edges are lightly browned (wedges will crisp upon standing).

2 Meanwhile, melt chocolate pieces and shortening in a small saucepan. Remove wedges from oven. Spread in an even layer on a serving platter; cool slightly. Drizzle with half of the melted chocolate mixture.

3 Arrange remaining wedges in a single layer on the same 15×10×1-inch baking pan. Bake as directed above. Spread in an even layer on a second serving platter; cool slightly. Drizzle with remaining melted chocolate mixture. Serve warm or cool.

Nutrition facts per wedge: 33 cal., 2 g total fat (1 g sat. fat), 2 mg chol., 22 mg sodium, 4 g carb., 0 g protein.

flan

Prep: 25 minutes
Bake: 35 minutes
Cool: 1 hour
Chill: 2 to 24 hours
Oven: 350°F
Makes: 8 servings

⅔ **cup sugar**

3 **eggs, beaten**

2 **egg yolks, beaten**

2 **cups whole milk**

1 **14-ounce can sweetened
condensed milk
(1⅓ cups)**

1 **tablespoon vanilla extract**

1 Preheat oven to 350°F. To caramelize sugar, in a heavy, large skillet cook sugar over medium-high heat until sugar begins to melt, shaking the skillet occasionally to heat the sugar evenly. Do not stir. Once the sugar starts to melt, reduce heat to low and cook about 5 minutes more or until all of the sugar is melted and golden, stirring as needed with a wooden spoon. Immediately pour the caramelized sugar into a 9×1½-inch round baking pan; using a pot holder, tilt the pan to coat the bottom of the pan evenly. Let stand for 10 minutes.

2 Meanwhile, combine the eggs, egg yolks, whole milk, sweetened condensed milk, and vanilla. Beat with a wire whisk until combined but not foamy. Place the baking pan in a large roasting pan on an oven rack. Pour the egg mixture into the baking pan. Pour boiling water into the roasting pan around the baking pan to a depth of ½ inch.

3 Bake for about 35 minutes or until a knife inserted near the center comes out clean. Remove pan from water. Cool on a wire rack for 1 hour. Cover and chill in refrigerator for at least 2 hours or up to 24 hours. To unmold flan, loosen edge with a flat metal spatula. Invert a round serving platter over the flan; turn baking pan and platter over together. Remove baking pan.

Nutrition facts per serving: 305 cal., 10 g total fat (5 g sat. fat), 158 mg chol., 119 mg sodium, 46 g carb., 10 g protein.

boca negra MINI CAKES

Prep: 30 minutes
Bake: 30 minutes
Cool: 10 minutes
Oven: 325°F
Makes: 8 servings

Butter

Sugar

1 **cup sugar**

⅓ **cup orange juice**

10 **ounces baking chocolate (56 to 62% cacao), finely chopped**

½ **cup butter**

4 **eggs**

4 **teaspoons all-purpose flour**

1 **to 2 teaspoons adobo sauce from canned chipotle chile peppers in adobo sauce**

¼ **teaspoon salt**

Sweet Crema*

1 Preheat oven to 325°F. Butter insides of eight 4- to 5-ounce ramekins and lightly coat with sugar.

2 In a medium saucepan, combine the 1 cup sugar and the orange juice. Bring to boiling over medium-high heat, stirring constantly. Remove from heat; add chocolate and the ½ cup butter, stirring until melted. Add eggs, one at a time, whisking well after each addition. Stir in flour, adobo sauce, and salt.

3 Place prepared ramekins in a 13×9×2-inch baking pan. Divide chocolate mixture evenly among the ramekins. Place baking pan on oven rack. Pour enough boiling water into the baking pan to reach halfway up the sides of the ramekins.

4 Bake for 30 to 35 minutes or until mixture is set (will not have a clean knife test). Using tongs, carefully remove ramekins from the water. Place on a wire rack; cool for 10 minutes. If desired, invert onto individual dessert plates. Serve warm with Sweet Crema.

***Sweet Crema:** In a small bowl, stir together ¾ cup Mexican crema or sour cream and ¼ cup sugar.

Nutrition facts per serving: 528 cal., 33 g total fat (19 g sat. fat), 152 mg chol., 221 mg sodium, 55 g carb., 6 g protein.

cinnamon churros
WITH MEXICAN CHOCOLATE DIPPING SAUCE

Prep: 30 minutes
Cool: 10 minutes
Cook: 2 minutes per batch
Oven: 300°F
Makes: about 20 churros

- **1 cup water**
- **⅓ cup butter**
- **2 tablespoons packed brown sugar**
- **½ teaspoon salt**
- **1 cup all-purpose flour**
- **1 egg**
- **½ teaspoon vanilla extract**
- **Vegetable oil for deep-fat frying**
- **¼ cup granulated sugar**
- **¾ teaspoon ground cinnamon**
- **¾ cup semisweet chocolate pieces**
- **¼ cup butter**
- **½ teaspoon ground pasilla or ancho chile pepper (optional)**
- **¼ teaspoon ground cinnamon**
- **⅔ cup granulated sugar**
- **1 5-ounce can evaporated milk (⅔ cup)**

1 In a medium saucepan, combine the water, the ⅓ cup butter, the brown sugar, and salt. Bring to boiling over medium heat. Add flour all at once, stirring vigorously with a wooden spoon. Cook and stir until mixture forms a ball and pulls away from the side of the pan. Remove from heat. Cool for 10 minutes. Add egg and vanilla, beating well with a wooden spoon.

2 Preheat oven to 300°F. Transfer mixture to a decorating bag fitted with a large open star tip. Line a baking sheet with waxed paper. Pipe 4×1-inch logs onto prepared baking sheet.

3 In a deep saucepan, heat 3 inches of oil to 375°F. Fry logs, a few at a time, in deep hot oil for about 2 minutes or until golden brown on both sides, turning once. Drain on paper towels. Keep warm in oven while cooking remaining churros.

4 In a medium bowl, combine the ¼ cup granulated sugar and the ¾ teaspoon cinnamon. Roll warm churros in cinnamon-sugar mixture to coat.

5 For Mexican chocolate dipping sauce, in a small saucepan combine chocolate pieces, the ¼ cup butter, the pasilla chile pepper (if desired), and the ¼ teaspoon cinnamon; cook and stir over medium heat until chocolate is melted. Add the ⅔ cup granulated sugar; gradually add the evaporated milk, stirring frequently to dissolve the sugar. Bring to boiling; reduce heat. Boil gently over low heat for 8 minutes, stirring frequently. Remove from heat. Cool slightly. Serve warm sauce with warm churros.

Nutrition facts per churro: 204 cal., 14 g total fat (5 g sat. fat), 27 mg chol., 109 mg sodium, 20 g carb., 2 g protein.

buñuelos

These puffy little doughnuts drizzled with a melted brown sugar and cinnamon sauce are an excellent choice for brunch.

Prep: 1 hour
Cook: 2 minutes per batch
Oven: 300°F
Makes: 24 buñuelos

2 **cups all-purpose flour**
1 **teaspoon baking powder**
½ **teaspoon salt**
¼ **teaspoon cream of tartar**
2 **tablespoons shortening**
2 **eggs, beaten**
⅓ **cup milk**
Cooking oil for frying
Brown Sugar Syrup* or Cinnamon Sugar**

1 In a large bowl, combine flour, baking powder, salt, and cream of tartar. Cut in shortening until mixture resembles coarse crumbs. Make a well in the center of the dry ingredients. In a small bowl, combine eggs and milk. Add to flour mixture all at once. Stir just until dough clings together.

2 On a lightly floured surface, knead dough for about 2 minutes or until soft and smooth. Divide dough into 24 equal portions. Shape each portion into a ball. Cover dough and let rest for 15 minutes.

3 Preheat oven to 300°F. In a heavy large skillet, heat about ¾ inch of cooking oil to 375°F. Meanwhile, on a lightly floured surface, roll each ball of dough to a 4-inch circle. Fry dough circles in hot oil about 1 minute on each side or until golden brown. Drain on paper towels. Keep buñuelos warm in oven while frying remaining dough. To serve, drizzle with Brown Sugar Syrup or sprinkle with Cinnamon Sugar.

*Brown-Sugar Syrup: In a small saucepan, combine 1 cup packed dark brown sugar and ½ cup water. Cook and stir over medium-high heat until sugar dissolves. Add 3 inches stick cinnamon or pinch ground cinnamon. Bring to boiling; reduce heat. Simmer, uncovered, for 5 minutes. Remove from heat. Stir in ½ teaspoon vanilla extract. Discard cinnamon stick. Serve warm. Makes ¾ cup syrup.

**Cinnamon Sugar: In a bowl, stir together ½ cup granulated sugar and 1 teaspoon ground cinnamon. Sprinkle over warm buñuelos.

Nutrition facts per buñuelo with syrup: 121 cal., 6 g total fat (1 g sat. fat), 18 mg chol., 69 mg sodium, 15 g carb., 2 g protein.

plantains WITH THICK CREAM

These caramelized plantains, seasoned with vanilla, cinnamon, and pecans, are topped with crema, a thickened cream mixture.

Start to Finish: 25 minutes
Makes: 4 servings

- **2** ripe medium plantains or 4 firm bananas
- **3** tablespoons butter or margarine
- **¼** cup packed brown sugar
- **1** teaspoon vanilla extract
- **¼** teaspoon ground cinnamon
- **2** tablespoons chopped pecans or walnuts or slivered almonds, toasted
- **½** cup Mexican crema, crème fraîche, or sour cream

1 Peel and bias-slice plantains or bananas into ½-inch-thick slices (about 2 cups).

2 Melt butter in a large skillet. Add plantains to melted butter. Heat for about 5 minutes for plantains (2 minutes for bananas) or just until warm and tender, gently stirring occasionally. Sprinkle with brown sugar. Stir gently until sugar melts.

3 Carefully stir in vanilla and cinnamon. Sprinkle with nuts. Serve immediately with crema.

Nutrition facts per serving: 358 cal., 22 g total fat (13 g sat. fat), 64 mg chol., 123 mg sodium, 41 g carb., 2 g protein.

metric information

The charts on this page provide a guide for converting measurements from the U.S. customary system, which is used throughout this book, to the metric system.

PRODUCT DIFFERENCES

Most of the ingredients called for in the recipes in this book are available in most countries. However, some are known by different names. Here are some common American ingredients and their possible counterparts:

- Sugar (white) is granulated, fine granulated, or castor sugar.
- Powdered sugar is icing sugar.
- All-purpose flour is enriched, bleached, or unbleached white household flour. When self-rising flour is used in place of all-purpose flour in a recipe that calls for leavening, omit the leavening agent (baking soda or baking powder) and salt.
- Light-colored corn syrup is golden syrup.
- Cornstarch is cornflour.
- Baking soda is bicarbonate of soda.
- Vanilla or vanilla extract is vanilla essence.
- Green, red, or yellow sweet peppers are capsicums or bell peppers.
- Golden raisins are sultanas.

VOLUME AND WEIGHT

The United States traditionally uses cup measures for liquid and solid ingredients. The chart, top right, shows the approximate imperial and metric equivalents. If you are accustomed to weighing solid ingredients, the following approximate equivalents will be helpful.

- 1 cup butter, castor sugar, or rice = 8 ounces = ½ pound = 250 grams
- 1 cup flour = 4 ounces = ¼ pound = 125 grams
- 1 cup icing sugar = 5 ounces = 150 grams

Canadian and U.S. volume for a cup measure is 8 fluid ounces (237 ml), but the standard metric equivalent is 250 ml.

1 British imperial cup is 10 fluid ounces.

In Australia, 1 tablespoon equals 20 ml, and there are 4 teaspoons in the Australian tablespoon.

Spoon measures are used for smaller amounts of ingredients. Although the size of the tablespoon varies slightly in different countries, for practical purposes and for recipes in this book, a straight substitution is all that's necessary. Measurements made using cups or spoons always should be level unless stated otherwise.

COMMON WEIGHT RANGE REPLACEMENTS

Imperial / U.S.	Metric
½ ounce	15 g
1 ounce	25 g or 30 g
4 ounces (¼ pound)	115 g or 125 g
8 ounces (½ pound)	225 g or 250 g
16 ounces (1 pound)	450 g or 500 g
1¼ pounds	625 g
1½ pounds	750 g
2 pounds or 2¼ pounds	1,000 g or 1 Kg

OVEN TEMPERATURE EQUIVALENTS

Fahrenheit Setting	Celsius Setting*	Gas Setting
300°F	150°C	Gas Mark 2 (very low)
325°F	160°C	Gas Mark 3 (low)
350°F	180°C	Gas Mark 4 (moderate)
375°F	190°C	Gas Mark 5 (moderate)
400°F	200°C	Gas Mark 6 (hot)
425°F	220°C	Gas Mark 7 (hot)
450°F	230°C	Gas Mark 8 (very hot)
475°F	240°C	Gas Mark 9 (very hot)
500°F	260°C	Gas Mark 10 (extremely hot)
Broil	Broil	Grill

*Electric and gas ovens may be calibrated using Celsius. However, for an electric oven, increase Celsius setting 10 to 20 degrees when cooking above 160°C. For convection or forced air ovens (gas or electric), lower the temperature setting 25°F/10°C when cooking at all heat levels.

BAKING PAN SIZES

Imperial / U.S.	Metric
9×1½-inch round cake pan	22- or 23×4-cm (1.5 L)
9×1½-inch pie plate	22- or 23×4-cm (1 L)
8×8×2-inch square cake pan	20×5-cm (2 L)
9×9×2-inch square cake pan	22- or 23×4.5-cm (2.5 L)
11×7×1½-inch baking pan	28×17×4-cm (2 L)
2-quart rectangular baking pan	30×19×4.5-cm (3 L)
13×9×2-inch baking pan	34×22×4.5-cm (3.5 L)
15×10×1-inch jelly roll pan	40×25×2-cm
9×5×3-inch loaf pan	23×13×8-cm (2 L)
2-quart casserole	2 L

U.S. / STANDARD METRIC EQUIVALENTS

⅛ teaspoon = 0.5 ml	⅓ cup = 3 fluid ounces = 75 ml
¼ teaspoon = 1 ml	½ cup = 4 fluid ounces = 125 ml
½ teaspoon = 2 ml	⅓ cup = 5 fluid ounces = 150 ml
1 teaspoon = 5 ml	¾ cup = 6 fluid ounces = 175 ml
1 tablespoon = 15 ml	1 cup = 8 fluid ounces = 250 ml
2 tablespoons = 25 ml	2 cups = 1 pint = 500 ml
¼ cup = 2 fluid ounces = 50 ml	1 quart = 1 liter

index

Note: Page references in *italics* refer to photographs.